Knowing Hyder personally, I can honestly say that he embodies the principles of his book, *Create Your Legacy: Four Portals to Living the Life of Love and Caring.* His ideas, stories, lessons and personal reflections embody generosity, gratitude, love and compassion. If you want to create your own magnificent legacy, read this book!

—Leonard Szymczak,
Author of *The Roadmap Home: Your GPS to Inner Peace*

This is an inspiring book written from the heart. Hyder is a man of integrity and wisdom and his book reflects his deep desire to help individuals discover their best lives. I highly recommend Dr. Hyder Zahed's book, *Create your Legacy: Four Portals to Living a Life of Love and Caring.*

~ Rev. Sandy Moore,
Author of *The Green Intention: Living in Sustainable Joy*

Rev. Sandy Moore
InSpirit Center for Spiritual Living
Mission Viejo, CA

CREATE
YOUR
LEGACY

Four Portals to Living a Life
of Love and Caring

DR. HYDER ZAHED

BALBOA
PRESS
A DIVISION OF HAY HOUSE

Balboa Press books may be ordered through booksellers or by contacting:

Balboa Press
A Division of Hay House
1663 Liberty Drive
Bloomington, IN 47403
www.balboapress.com
1-(877) 407-4847

Because of the dynamic nature of the Internet, any web addresses or links contained in this book may have changed since publication and may no longer be valid. The views expressed in this work are solely those of the author and do not necessarily reflect the views of the publisher, and the publisher hereby disclaims any responsibility for them.

The author of this book does not dispense medical advice or prescribe the use of any technique as a form of treatment for physical, emotional, or medical problems without the advice of a physician, either directly or indirectly. The intent of the author is only to offer information of a general nature to help you in your quest for emotional and spiritual well-being. In the event you use any of the information in this book for yourself, which is your constitutional right, the author and the publisher assume no responsibility for your actions.

Any people depicted in stock imagery provided by Thinkstock are models, and such images are being used for illustrative purposes only. Certain stock imagery © Thinkstock.

Printed in the United States of America.

ISBN: 978-1-4525-8029-6 (sc)
ISBN: 978-1-4525-8030-2 (hc)
ISBN: 978-1-4525-8031-9 (e)

Library of Congress Control Number: 2013914998

Balboa Press rev. date: 10/29/2013

DEDICATION

For my beloved parents and their unfailing
loving kindness and generosity

and for

my beautiful daughter, Auria, without whose
love, support and encouragement, I would
not have completed my Legacy!

ACKNOWLEDGEMENTS

I WOULD LIKE TO EXPRESS my deepest appreciation and gratitude to all those who provided me the support to complete this book. A special gratitude I give to my friends Jay and Gabriella Cole whose moral support and encouragement helped me coordinate my thoughts in writing this book. Furthermore, I would also like to acknowledge with much appreciation Laura Bollinger and Christy Hummer for their editing expertise and suggestions; my friend Leonard Szymczak who encouraged me to write from my heart and to share my inner voice with my readers. My thanks are also due to Chan Minh for his photographic input.

I owe my thanks also to Kathy Juline who reviewed my book, provided me with helpful comments and suggestions and shared some valuable affirmations on love, generosity, gratitude and compassion which the readers will find condensed at the end of the book. Many thanks are also due to my friends Duncan and Shannon for their ongoing loving support and friendship; Fatima Khan for reviewing the manuscript and offering some additional insights; and my friend Doug Godsman who inspired me to redesign my life. Last but not the least my special appreciation and thanks to Angenieta Wuerth for helping me with the design of the book cover.

CONTENTS

INTRODUCTION

Shifting Life

A FEW YEARS BACK, I not only thought my life was good, but I also would have said it was great. I enjoyed good health, a happy marriage, a beautiful daughter, a comfortable home, a wonderful community, and meaningful work. Then one day, quite out of the blue, came a shocking thunderbolt. While getting ready for a business trip to Europe, my wife informed me that she had decided not to return home this time! At first I thought I did not hear her correctly. Maybe the statement was incomplete or she was going to tell me she was coming back later or earlier than planned. That was not the case. She was clearly stating that our twenty-year marriage was ending soon. Perhaps it was the shock of the statement, or maybe there wasn't enough time to get into a lengthy discussion, but nothing more was said. I was left behind to process the end of my deeply cherished family life.

After the shock, I immersed myself in the demands of work. I worked in the research and development department of a major pharmaceutical company, and I felt good about my contribution in finding cures for diseases and illnesses. I continued my daily workout regimen and tried to remain positive.

As I was trying to cope with the impending disintegration of my family, I was struck with more disastrous news, this time from my supervisor. He informed me that due to a corporate reorganization, my department was being dissolved; 450 employees, including me, were being let go. Once again, I was speechless. Quietly I left the meeting, handed my badge to the security guard, and wished him well. I recall sitting in my car, feeling like this was all surreal, and just trying to process my job loss. I was in so much pain. I had lost my marriage and my job. I wondered what was to come next.

The next day I would wake up not knowing what to do with my day. There would be no structure, no expectations, and no purpose. Though I was in a state of shock, I knew I must reach out for help.

I called my friend Doug and shared with him what had transpired at work that morning. He said quietly, "I can hear in your voice that this is serious. Stay where you are. I'll come over within thirty minutes." When he arrived, he suggested, "Let's go out for breakfast so we can talk."

As I began to describe what had just taken place that morning, I felt my emotions beginning to loosen as my words flowed out spontaneously. Sitting at the table over scrambled eggs and toast, Doug listened with care and understanding, giving me the empathetic support I needed with his caring words of wisdom.

I'll never forget one important insight he shared during that breakfast: "Hyder, this is your chance to redesign your life. As a career counselor, I have known many people who have taken a major loss like this, survived it, and changed their lives along the lines of what they truly want to accomplish in the aftermath. Years later, looking back, they have seen that the loss turned out to be the best thing that ever happened to them."

While Doug was talking, I kept remembering a line from Hafiz, one of my favorite Sufi poets: "Before a breakthrough, there is always a breakdown." As I revisited these wise words of the ancient Persian mystic, I felt a mixture of sorrow, hope, and fear.

To move forward toward redesigning my life, Doug told me to make a list of the things I really wanted to do before I die. I knew right then this list would become the blueprint of the new life I was supposed to design. I started with a list of all the things I hadn't been able to do because of my former work demands. This was my list.

1. Spend more time with family and friends.
2. Travel.
3. Learn to fly an airplane.

Indeed, within that first week, I joined a flying club. I did this while I was still going through the grieving process, unable to sleep soundly, and having obsessive thoughts about what went wrong. I wondered how I might suddenly have been of no value to my former employer, but at least I had initiated one concept in my new life design.

I was resolved to move forward with zeal and perseverance despite the two recent major setbacks. I worked out at the gym, kept myself well groomed and tried to make my new daily experiences as meaningful as possible in an attempt to keep my spirits high. Little did I know, that the 'grand finale' of this set of trials was about to play out.

One day while working out at the gym, I felt some discomfort in my left arm, and as quick as a lightning bolt, I was unconscious. When I came around, all I could make out were the blurry faces of paramedics working around me and the shrill sound of an ambulance siren.

Later, a young doctor approached me and asked me if I knew what was happening. I told him, judging by the tone of the paramedics in the ambulance; all I knew was that it was something serious, not much more. The doctor matter-of-factly said, "Mr. Zahed, you are having a heart attack. You are very a lucky man because the gym staff called for help immediately. Now you are in good hands."

Within a short time, the nurses changed my clothes, transferred me onto a stretcher, and had me moved to a pre-op room in preparation for a coronary angiography and insertion of stents into my arteries.

This time when I regained consciousness, I saw a nurse hooking me up to an IV drip. Three monitors faithfully flashed my vital signs with silent beeps and bright waves of light across their screens. In the intensive care ward, my reality revolved around the bed, the light-green curtains drawn around me, the monitors, my weak body, and not much more. The medications made me go into a deep sleep, deep enough for my mind to create colorful dreams of my entire life.

My life, from my earliest memories, flashed in my deep consciousness. When I awakened intermittently, questions arose such as, "Who am I? Where did I come from? Where am I going? What is my life all about?" and most importantly, "What exactly is the purpose of my life?" I recounted all the things in my life that had not changed: I still had a beautiful daughter; I still had family and friends who loved and cared about me, not so much in the role of a married man or an executive with a good degree, but *me* as a human being. All I knew was that I wanted to live, and that if I did, I would be committed to making sure my life counted, that I would make a positive difference in the bigger picture, that I would leave a legacy of goodness behind, and that I would live a meaningful, beneficial life.

When I returned home after the hospital stay, I began to think about redesigning my life. A small piece of paper became a gentle foundation for the design, a handwritten entry from my late mother's diary. A couple of years after my mother passed away, my two sisters were looking through her possessions, deciding what to give away and what to keep. In the closet, they came across a small diary through which, out of curiosity, they began to browse, flipping the pages, pausing to read here and there. One page caught their eye; it was an entry about me. She had written about how much happiness I had brought into her life, how I had never talked back or raised my voice to her. Essentially, she was honoring me by reciting the little things I had done to give her joy. The page ended with prayers and blessings for me now and in the afterlife.

Immediately my sisters made a photocopy and sent it to me. As I read it, I felt the simplicity and sincerity of her words. The journal entry wasn't a reaction to having received a nice gift, card, or phone call from me. It wasn't intended to impress anyone or to ask a favor. It was just a note jotted down during her quiet moments as she mused privately over our relationship as mother and son. It was merely an evanescent acknowledgment passing through her heart, penned onto the pages of her private diary. I folded it carefully and tucked it away in a special spot so I could retrieve it during difficult and discouraging times in my life when I might need some uplifting. I now cherish this little document as the very best letter of recommendation I have ever received, among a file folder of accolades from high-level management over the years.

Certainly, this was one of those difficult and discouraging moments. I got out that little folded page and read it in silence. I knew it was my mother's heartfelt legacy to me. Sensing the power of gratitude and love she was bequeathing me in her words, I began to ask, "What is mine to leave behind for my loved ones?" Thus I began to contemplate not only what I wanted to do with the rest of my life but also what I wanted to be in my relationships and how I wanted my friends and family to remember me. This was a poignant moment of awakening to the question of what I was supposed to leave behind as my own personal gift, my most valuable contribution, my legacy.

Considering a Legacy

It was then that I decided that I would jot down my thoughts, my life experience. I would define for myself and for my child who I was and from what foundation I had always approached life. Like my mother before me, I wanted to leave her with some of my cherished thoughts. Additionally, I would no longer take the love, generosity, and compassion of my family and friends for granted. The time had come for me to not only redesign my life, as my good friend Doug had suggested, but also to acknowledge all the great favors providence had bestowed upon me. The following pages reflect the musings of an ordinary man who came to live a good life, only to have it erased in a matter of a short passage of time—a man who is now resolved to seek the true meaning of existence, who is embarking on a journey to discover for himself the true purpose of life to make a difference.

I began to conduct research about leaving a legacy and discovered an exercise in *The Seven Habits of Highly Effective People* by Steven Covey to help detect and clarify our true values and how we would want to be remembered.

He says to:

1. Imagine walking into your memorial service.
2. Notice four speakers in your service—one from your family, a second from among your friends, a third from your work associates, and a fourth from your acquaintances in some community organization.
3. Consider what you would like to have each one say about you.
4. Take your time to hear what each speaker is sharing about you, one by one, sentence by sentence. (As you imagine them speaking, you are hearing an articulation of your deepest held values in these four sectors of your life. If these comments feel good to you and are what you sincerely would like to hear said about you, then you know it is time to start being aware of the need to make any changes that may be required in order to go in the direction you wish to go, if you aren't already. (Covey 1989).

I went through the exercise and thought about what I valued the most. I didn't value leaving material possessions behind, even though leaving them behind is not a bad idea. However, my list included that which anyone from any walk of life could leave: love, generosity, gratitude, and compassion. Still, though, after considering what kind of legacy I wanted to leave behind, I realized I was still facing myself and my negative thoughts and feelings.

Overcoming Emotional Darkness

While I was in the emotional darkness, I could either hide and stubbornly isolate myself behind my fear and anger or choose to look up through the dark cloud and glimpse some sunshine through the haze. I decided to try an ancient *Tibetan Buddhist practice adapted from Guided Meditations for Difficult Times: A Lamp in the Darkness* by Jack Kornfield. The practice is supposed to help people through dark moments. The steps include:

> Think of something in your life that feels dark and discouraging, something that seems like a blockage.

> Imagine this something is a big dark cushion that you're sitting upon. (It could even be somewhat comfortable sinking down into the dark pillow underneath you. But after a while, you feel ready to make a change.)

> Arise, pick up the cushion and thrust it into the sky where it suddenly becomes a big, dark

cloud. (So you've already made progress: you're now looking at the obstacle out there rather than letting it be the foundation of your life.)

Just gaze at the cloud until little-by-little you notice a tiny opening that reveals the clear, blue sky behind the cloud. (Keep watching that tiny opening. Whenever your mind's eye wanders back to the dark cloud, just gently and lovingly draw your attention back to the bright opening. Gradually the opening gets bigger and bigger, without any forcefulness on your part. It just easily grows wider and wider as you gaze at the tiny hole; you see more and more of the open sky.)

Keep watching until the cloud has entirely dissipated and only the pure blue light of the sky fills your mind. (This practice may take minutes or hours. Also, you may need to keep coming back to the image. Once you succeed in seeing the fullness and emptiness of the vast, clear sky, when thoughts of a dark cloud pop up, simply go back to the image of the open sky, over and over again. (Kornfield 2010)

This practice truly helped me with my internal dialogue and helped me to move forward through the darkness.

Contemplating the Law of Emergence

I continued my research to help me continue to move forward in my new life design. Ralph Waldo Emerson, the American transcendentalist thinker, wrote that the ancestor of every action is a thought.

In his book, *Make Your Life Worthwhile, published in* 1946, the great theologian Emmet Fox writes that there are really only two feelings into which all the seeming varieties of feelings reduce themselves: "All other feelings will turn out (upon analysis) to be either love or fear." Anger, hatred, jealousy, and criticism, for instance, are various manifestations of our fears. On the other hand, joy, interest, success, accomplishment, and appreciation are various forms of love. Fox elaborates further and says love is a creative emotion while fear is a destructive emotion. Love rebuilds, inspires, expands, and opens the way while fear harms and paralyzes the body making all things lack pallor.

The ancient Taoists, contemporary films and books such as *The Secret* by Rhonda Byrne express the law of attraction. The law of attraction is the belief that "like attracts like" and by focusing on positive or negative thoughts, one can bring about positive or negative results. We can choose to focus on love or on fear.

Upon contemplating on this law for myself, I decided to think of it as the 'Law of Emergence'. This law is my reality in that I no longer need to expend my energy in trying to attract what exists outside of me, but rather I need to focus on awakening, nurturing, and fostering my own inner emotions and thoughts. From now on, this would constitute my personal reality in the realm in which I chose to exist.

Committing to a Good Life

From the law of emergence that my inner ideas and feelings will emerge as realities in my life, I decided to commit to living a good life, a life I sincerely desired to live, by breaking away from my old habits of reacting mindlessly from old, unconscious patterns. I decided that as an adult, it was time to set my own standards for my life. I wanted to live by what I knew to be true by making choices from my innermost ideas and feelings.

Of course, this book, as a tangible legacy, is my exploration of what I believe are profoundly important values for the uplifting of our human experience through promoting greater love, generosity, gratitude, and compassion. What really counts is whether, and to what degree, I practice these values in my daily life. That is the true application of these virtues. That is my true legacy. Have I been able to put into practice what I care about, especially in my more difficult relationships and sectors of my daily life?

My mother, I recalled, was the most loving and grateful person I have ever known. I remember her as a truly happy person who didn't complain or condemn or hold grudges.

She was fun-loving and playful; she was grateful for even the tiniest things. If a child picked a wildflower and handed it to her, her eyes sparkled with pleasure and appreciation. She cherished that little weed the same as the most costly bouquet of cultivated hothouse roses. I realized that her legacy to me was love and gratitude.

When I thought of my father, the qualities that came immediately to mind were his generosity and compassion. He didn't have to give us children lectures about these qualities. All we had to do was watch him write out requests for money orders at the breakfast table first thing in the morning on the day he received his month's paycheck. To this moment, I still don't know exactly what process he was following, but I do know now that he was giving a portion of his income to people and organizations he chose to help. The remainder of his pay would then be deposited into our family's bank account. I also remember him stuffing treats into his pockets anytime he left the house. As we walked out of our house, he would reach into his pocket and grab a tidbit to give to children who were our neighbors. Seeing a smile brighten a child's little face put a smile deep in his heart.

I grew up witnessing on a daily basis the qualities of love, generosity, gratitude, and compassion in the way my parents lived. Those immeasurable qualities, which were truly the flavor and atmosphere of my early life, became the intangible legacy my parents left for me. Today, as an adult, I can treasure their example even more because I have gone through a somber period of disappointment, loss, and health challenges.

The legacy that was passed on to me by my parents forms the acronym LGGC, and if I chose to pronounce them together, phonetically the acronym takes on the sound of the word, "legacy". This discovery was profound in itself. As I jotted down the initials of these four qualities—LGGC—I noticed something profound. The letters LGGC were actually an acronym, which, when spoken aloud, became the word *legacy*.

Every person has the ability to make his/her values practical in personal and unique ways. The famous child psychologist Eric Erickson is of the opinion that children learn a lot more from observing the actions and behaviors of their primary role models (parents), when compared to rules and expectations parents impart to them verbally. The same is true for LGGC. It's always easier to carry on an interesting intellectual discussion about these ideas than to actually exercise them during moments of intense personal difficulty in a relationship with loved ones, coworkers at the office, or people who cross our paths every day.

My dream is that each reader will be inspired to make positive, life-affirming changes in the various areas of their lives for greater happiness and contentment. Moment by moment, day by day, I keep taking little opportunities to be more loving, generous, grateful, and compassionate. Little by little, I feel a deeper sense of satisfaction and freedom in situations where I once felt frustrated, discouraged, or uncertain about what to do. With each practical choice, I am more firmly committed to living my LGGC; with each positive choice, I feel stronger and happier than ever before.

After further thought, I formed a circular diagram of these four principles:

Putting LGGC into Action

There's no set direction for the flow of energy or any particular place where the circle begins or ends. At any given moment, we can enter into the magnetic field of these principles through any opening or portal.

In one situation, for instance, we might not be able to feel the warmth and closeness characteristic of the emotion of love, but we could still feel compassion. Take the example of a mother with a son who has been using heroin. She might not be able to feel coziness or the desire for closeness due to his emotional distance and numbness from the use of the drug. The mother wouldn't feel happy that her son is sleeping all throughout the day and then acting grouchy and angry as the drug begins to wear off. Yet she could still feel compassion for what her son is going through and thus be able to enter through that portal.

Soon she might be able to touch the generosity deep inside her and thereby muster enough energy to reach out and help her son get the medical help and emotional support he needs. If she can't feel love, compassion, or generosity, then she might be able to feel gratitude for the good things in her life. It's relatively easy to do that, but we don't want to stop there.

What I'm offering is a different way of ranging through the repertoire of possible responses other than flip-flopping back and forth between the opposite polarities of love or fear; kindness or rudeness; peace or anger; serenity or violence; compassion or numbness; intimacy or coldness. If I can't feel love at this moment, then I don't have to resort to anger, bitterness, coldness, disdain, or cruelty. Instead, we can feel compassion, which is essentially a sense of poignant awareness of the pain the other person must be experiencing. That will be a good beginning for a healthier direction for us personally as well as for the relationship itself.

If we can't feel generous-hearted right now for whatever reason, we can go to the portal of gratitude and begin to recite what we're grateful for in our lives. There's always a portal I can enter if I look for it. Then the experience of appreciation can stimulate a sense of expanded generosity and openness. Any one of the domains can open the way to any of the others and on and on. Essentially, I start wherever I am at the moment and go from there.

One thing I know for sure is that whatever I intend to leave as my legacy in the future will influence how I live my life in the present. Feelings and thoughts are just good ideas. Our deepest-held beliefs and values are merely wonderful possibilities— until they are put into action. The LGGC (legacy) model I designed was my new design for life. This design included a circle because life is often referred to as the circle of life.

I organized this book by dividing it into four chapters based on the LGGC acronym. Therefore chapter one is Love, chapter two Generosity and so on. The main content of each of these chapters are my reflections on the topic, my real-life experiences, followed by a summary of the chapter and finally a list of key points to remember and refer to with ease in the future. *Create Your Legacy* concludes with summary and sources for further research.

Note to readers: The following pages include research and real-life examples of each of the characteristics I hope to share with others and pass onward for many generations to come as my legacy. It is my hope that you will consider putting LGGC (legacy) into action into your life because doing so will exponentially improve your life and the lives of others.

CHAPTER ONE

Love

"Love is a force more formidable than any other.
It is invisible-it cannot be seen or measured,
yet it is powerful enough to transform you
in a moment, and offer you more joy
than any material possession could."
(Barbara de Angelis)

LOVE IN THE LGGC (LEGACY) model is the first and most-complex principle. However, it, like all the other portals, can be accessed at any time. First we need to gain knowledge of different types of love so we can understand what we seek to access. We can learn much about the complexity and types of love from the ancient Greeks. In the Greek language, more than one word describes love.

Eros describes love that changes from moment to moment based on varying circumstances. For example, when love partners are expressing pleasing words and treating each other with passion, the warm, fuzzy feeling of love grows, and the desire to spend time together increases. But, when the partners are negative or share painful words, they may pull away and choose to spend less time together.

What causes us to consciously pull away? Let's think about it. People want to avoid pain and move toward what they perceive to be pleasure. We not only withdraw from pain or negative emotions in romantic relationships, but we also withdraw in all other types of relationships, whether with family, coworkers, friends, or acquaintances. When we withdrawal, *Eros* love dissipates because it is love based upon external pain/pleasure circumstances.

Good news! There are options if we want sustainable relationships. First, we have to expand our understanding of love to extend beyond Eros and consider love a virtuous principle.

Love as a Virtue

If we want a kind of love that is enduring and steady under all circumstances, we can choose *agape* love. Agape love is often referred to as a general affection or deeper sense of true love or sacrificial love. This kind of love honors others regardless of whether the circumstances are pleasant and whether others satisfy us or meet our expectations and desires.

To move toward enduring love, I challenge you to think of love as a virtue rather than as an emotion. *Namaste* from the

Hindu tradition means, "I acknowledge the spirit within you as the same spirit within me." This kind of love involves a commitment to stay aware of our oneness with others and all life. Even if someone has a difficult personality or flawed character or if circumstances are not easy, we can still honor that person from the spiritual perspective because in essence, we are all made of the same spirit.

When we are experiencing life-constricting emotions (e.g., anger, fear) that seem contrary to maintaining a loving relationship, all love is not lost. We can turn our attention to the principle of love and choose to enter that portal. Love calls us to treat others with respect and kindness and to speak gently, even when we don't like what they are doing or saying or how they look or think. Loving another under difficult circumstances is respecting the other person's divinity, which is the same as ours.

Brother Ishmael Tetteh is a contemporary African mystic and spiritual speaker from Ghana author of the book *The Way Forward: Principles and Practices for Practical Living*, his main claim in this book is—"Love is not a sentiment; it is a discipline." We must discipline ourselves to remember that none of us is outside the spirit of life; none of us is really alone. When we insist on remembering this truth of our oneness, we can honor the divinity of others. When we do so, we are acting out of the principle of love. (Tetteh 2005).

Loving emotions are valuable expressions and experiences of human life. The truth is that when we regard others from the perspective of the unchanging principle of oneness, then relationships are strengthened and made more beautiful and powerful. It is up to us in our vision of oneness to give love. Dr. River Smith, in his striking book *A Conspiracy to Love*, succinctly says, "We don't find love by seeking it; we find love by giving it." When we give love, let's choose to give it unconditionally. (Smith 2009).

Unconditional Love

Unconditional love is treating the other person with kindness and respect, even when the conditions or circumstances don't appear to warrant such actions. In his book, *Real Love (2003)*, Dr. Greg Baer explores the destructive effects of conditional love. Conditional love starts with how our parents expressed their acceptance or rejection of our behavior. If we did something pleasing, helpful, or smart, our parents or other influential adults would smile and speak to us in a tone of joy with a feeling of approval. They would typically say, "Good job!" or "Way to go!" when we made a high grade on our math quiz or picked up our scattered toys. We had met our parents' conditions to express their appreciation of us. In turn, we felt loved and wanted.

On the other hand, when we did something unpleasing, rough, inconvenient, or seemingly stupid, our parents might frown, roll their eyes, sigh heavily, giving us the feeling that we were not loved when we displeased them. The child simply didn't meet the condition(s) required to get the parents' loving approval. Because of this, we may go through life thinking that feeling loved comes from doing something to earn the approval of another person. Some children may experience love as an ever-changing, unstable, and conditional emotion.

Johannes Bourgeois, a teacher of science of the mind, used to ask students to rephrase the common expression, "I deserve love." She taught that as long as we think we have to deserve love, we'll never experience ourselves as worthy and valuable. Instead, try saying, "I am the presence of love" or "My relationships are centers of love" or "I bring love with me wherever I go." Having to deserve love leads to people-pleasing and courtship rather than the relaxation of simply knowing we are here to give love, receive love, and be a loving presence.

A mother asking for help regarding her relationship with her son was in a counseling session with Rev. Beckwith, a contemporary new thought speaker and writer. The mother said, "I don't know why my son in prison feels so distant from me. I visit him regularly, put money on his books, and I always remember to close every visit by saying, 'Honey, remember—I love you, no matter what.'" Beckwith urged her to slightly change the sentence next time. "Just leave off the last part and see if that makes a difference," he said. At the end of the next visit, the mother did just that. She said simply, "Honey, remember—I love you." She noticed a subtle expression in her son's eyes that seemed surprised, somehow softer. Over time, the communication between them improved. The "no matter what" had been a reminder of all the unacceptable, disappointing things he had done in the past. This little phrase had been undermining the feeling of genuine unconditional love his mother really felt inside. (Beckwith 2013 E-source)

Dr. Baer insists that if we identify love with meeting the expectations or conditions of our parents or others, then as children and adults we will demand that others please us and meet up to our needs and expectations. We perpetuate the cycle of unhappiness brought on by the conditional love we are using in our own relationships. We keep blaming our unhappiness on our partner, our children, our siblings, our friends, or others. We are unaware that our own conditional loving mode (inherited from our upbringing) is what is destroying our present happiness and setting up our current relationships for frustration and failure. Once we understand the vicious pain/pleasure cycle, we can begin the necessary transformation toward loving unconditionally, toward experiencing "real love." By regarding and treating others with respect, we stand on the solid ground of principle rather than on passing emotions and temporary conditions.

Self-Love and Respect

Having respect for others is not possible unless we have respect for ourselves. By respect, naturally, I don't mean being impressed by our own title, status, position, or appearance. I mean honoring our inner divine being. In Christianity, Mark 12:31 says to love your neighbor as yourself.

We must first love and respect ourselves before we can truly give love and respect to our neighbors. Daylee Deanna Schwartz urges us in her book, *How Do I Love Me*, to get out of the habit of focusing on shortcomings and get into the habit of giving positive qualities more attention. (Schwartz 2012).

To build self-love and overcome low self-esteem is to change how we feel emotionally about ourselves. To change our emotion requires changing two different core beliefs about self-image. The first core belief that hinders self-love is a false belief that we are not good enough. The second false core belief is that we are not who we should be. We can have self-love and self-respect if we know we are good enough to do what we are meant to do. We can in any moment decide who we want to be and take action. If we choose to be more loving, we can start with loving-kindness.

Loving-Kindness

Treating ourselves and others with loving-kindness starts with speaking gently and politely, in a manner that communicates respect. Showing kindness to others is possible when we have made a commitment to practice loving-kindness and well-wishing regardless of the difficulty or disappointment of the situation. Moreover, treating others with kindness has the potential to bring out the best in others rather than the worst. Thus, showing kindness increases the chances of improving relationships and situations.

Gary Chapman, who is not only a writer and workshop facilitator but also a minister and family counselor, suggests occasionally making a list in the evening of all the instances of kindness we have experienced that day. These instances can come through the actions or words of others or from us. For example, a neighbor I had never met before rang my doorbell and told me that the interior lights were on in a truck parked in front of my house. It just so happened the truck belonged to a friend who was visiting me. My friend and I were truly grateful for the kind communication. Each entry of thought of loving-kindness doesn't have to be momentous or world-shaking.

Maintaining a kindness list helps us become more aware of our own progress toward becoming more loving and giving under all circumstances. Such increased awareness may prompt us to have the courage to go back and apologize to another person when we have been unkind. In addition, increased awareness helps us view every interaction with others as an opportunity to express kindness deliberately. The sincere intention of practicing the principle of Namaste in all of our relationships is what we usually call unconditional love.

Honesty

Celebrating ourselves, our relationships, and life itself is not possible without honesty. When we are dishonest with others, either by verbal falsehood or by presenting a false image, we are living a lie. If we are dishonest, then we are not honoring and celebrating life; indeed, we are defiling life. Lying to others is a sure way to put distance between us and undermine the foundation of any relationship. Truthfulness with others builds mutual trust and creates a sense of openness and spaciousness to exist in the friendship, thus cultivating a feeling of safety and comfort. The toll of dishonesty is distrust and isolation. The reward of honesty is deepening our connections with all others, taking responsibility for our own actions, and strengthening our own self-worth and esteem.

Thich Nhat Hanh, a contemporary Buddhist monk and global peace worker, in his book *Being Peace* (2005) writes that speaking honestly in any negotiation between individuals or groups is necessary. Speaking the truth in a loving way is also necessary. He says to use only "loving speech" when communicating about our differences and disagreements. We must be lovingly honest; we must discipline ourselves to speak in a way that conveys respect, gentleness, and humility.

Gary Chapman in *Love as a Way of Life* (2009) uses the vivid metaphor of words as being either bullets or seeds. If we use our words as bullets with a feeling of superiority and condemnation, we are not going to be able to restore a relationship to love. If we use our words as seeds with a feeling of supportiveness and sincere goodwill, we can rebuild relationships in positive and life-affirming ways.

When we need to open up and talk candidly about something difficult with another person, we must set aside time to focus on the conversation with keen attention and purpose. During the conversation, we must listen patiently, speak tactfully, and tell the truth as we understand it. We must align our words, voice inflection and tone, eye expression, body language, and actions with our inner awareness in our honest exchange.

One of the best ways to enrich and deepen the love in any relationship is to develop the habit of honesty in both little and big matters. Honesty may not always be comfortable. If honest communication is the norm rather than the exception in our relationships, we are freeing ourselves and others to be authentic.

Balancing Love Relationships and Work

Being fully present, whether at home, in love relationships, or at work, can be challenging. However, it is necessary to fully experience the principle of love.

A woman who felt she did not receive enough fatherly love recently told me that her father, who had been a CEO with a leading company in Europe, provided every material want she and her two brothers had during their childhood. However, with his heavy responsibilities at work, she and her siblings almost never saw him. She remembered one time when he had to attend a major conference in Hawaii. He took all three children with him, set them up in a big, beautiful room in a luxurious hotel, and then left them alone while he participated in the conference throughout the day and evening. Later, his daughter had the courage to tell her father they would have preferred to stay at home where they could at least play with their friends in the neighborhood. He was shocked. Naturally, he thought he was doing a wonderful thing by taking his children along even though he knew he would have to leave them while he worked many hours during the week. He had failed to balance his love for his children with his work requirements because he was not truly present with his children.

Being Truly Present

We may be physically present, of course, without being emotionally or mentally present. Sometimes we may text or check our smartphones while others are talking with us. We may do this even if what we're aiming for in the portal of love is a sense of being fully present, listening, responding, paying attention, enjoying each other's presence, and conveying a positive regard to others.

The only time we are alive is in the present moment. The present moment is all we have. The past is a memory, and the future is an idea, a possibility. Like the CEO who took his children to Hawaii but didn't have time for them, we often become aware of sad insights of not being present after the fact. We can't go back and recapture the past, so when we get an opportunity to be truly present, we don't want to lose it.

In my own life, I struggled with being truly present. For example, as a supervisor in a fast-paced, competitive corporate world, I struggled with balancing home and work demands. Yet, one day I wrote a simple note to my daughter that she cherishes to this day.

Honey,

I am with you, around you, for you, and beside you—always.

Dad

I have worked to find a balance as often as I could between being away at work and being present at home. Often pulling away was neither convenient nor easy when I was tempted to finish one more step of a major project even though my daughter was yearning for my presence at home. I needed discipline and determination to balance my desire to provide with my desire to share my unconditional love and time. When conflicted with competing desires, we can choose to be fully present and to act from the portal of love.

Patient Love

A worthy goal is to become ever more patient in our relationships to express love. Buddha taught that patience is the gatekeeper between the two worlds of our unconscious impulses and our conscious choices. Patience can close the gate on harmful impulses that are constantly pushing their way up from the layer of hidden conditioned habits or patterns in every cell. Reactive, mindless behaviors try to take over and are sure to bring harm to our relationships and our health. These behaviors reenact the trauma experienced in our childhood, trauma that made us feel powerless, worthless, unlovable, or alone. Patient love can help us to stop repeating the trauma that we have known in our past.

Love Requires Action

Mark, a young man twenty years of age, recently took his own life. He had been extremely active in the youth program at his church and was well loved by the teens and their families, his peers, the youth program directors, and the ministers. More than seven hundred people attended his memorial service, which was held late on a Friday afternoon. The minister spoke the truth when he said that he was certain that everyone present sincerely loved Mark. However, he asked how many of us had actually expressed that love and appreciation to Mark himself while he was still alive. Too many times we take for granted that our friends and loved ones know how much we cherish them and how grateful we are to have them in our lives. He estimated that nine out of ten people probably did not actively share with Mark how dearly they loved and appreciated him. Let us express our love clearly while the other person is still alive, not waiting to express our thoughts to their families after they are gone. When we remain mindful of the law of impermanence, we cherish each moment as though it were the last. We must remember to tell and show others that we truly love them.

In relationships, we can look upon every disappointment or conflict as an opportunity to give even greater love rather than retaliating in anger. Dr. Gerald Jampolsky, psychiatrist and founder of the Center for Attitudinal Healing, said that every act is either a call from love or a call for love. It's up to us to respond to every call for love from love. Every interaction in every new moment is an invitation to practice greater love and support.

Water as a Symbol of Love

Supportiveness and reliability, as depicted by and encouraged in the amazingly effective work of Dr. Jampolsky's program, remind me of the qualities of water. I think of water as the symbol for love because water is universal. Water goes everywhere, seeps into everything. No matter how hardened a substance may be water will soften it. In the words of Matthew Fox, there is no problem, however complex and difficult, that enough love cannot dissolve.

Water runs into the tiniest and most lowly places. When we love others unconditionally, we take the humble position of supporting them, of truly wanting them to be happy rather than seeking self-aggrandizement. As mentioned above, Paul in his often-quoted letter to the Corinthians said that love is not boastful and puffed up; rather, love is kind and humble.

Water is patient because it persistently wears away even the hardest granite mountain over millions of years, flushing the rock's minerals downstream to the ocean. St. Paul also said love is patient and long-suffering. Unconditional loving allows us to wait, to take time, to be steady and still, to know only the best during intense moments, to have faith in the innate goodness of the other person and us, to believe that a positive, life-affirming outcome is always possible.

Water purifies and cleanses just by washing over anything, clearing away the silt and calcified residue by virtue of simply being itself, by moving freely and continuously. Love is like that too. When a problem or misunderstanding arises, communication expressed from a gentle tide of kindness and openness has a cleansing effect so people can feel the safety of releasing and sharing what's really troubling them. This releasing opens the way for reconciliation.

It is believed that our emotions are carried in the water of our bodies—our tears, sweat, blood, and moist breath. The body shows a state of balance and good health when our water flow is unobstructed. Circulation of our feelings in life-affirming ways is like the circulation of water that keeps the pond of life fresh and clean, yielding ever greater life. Water is nourishing as it brings nutrients to the dry field to allow sprouting and blossoming for an abundant harvest. Like water, love is the great nurturer.

So too is love like water. Love is the natural medium that carries messages, that flows incessantly and silently, bringing us together, conveying what is often unspoken—the message from our hearts to others and to the world—allowing life to continue and flourish in all our relationships.

Relishing Our Connections

Love flourishes in our relationships when we take time to appreciate each precious moment we have with our loved ones. Over the years, I made sure I set aside time for playfulness and closeness with my daughter. For example, during her childhood bedtime on most evenings, we would cuddle up and read one or two stories; then we would play Boat before saying goodnight. Boat consisted of bouncing vigorously on the bed so that the mattress shook as if it were a fragile vessel in a stormy sea. Auria, my daughter, would scream, "Shark!" or "Man overboard!" as we peered over the side of the boat into the violently churning ocean waves.

Mind you, I wasn't forcing myself to play these games; I was having fun! I was immersed in the play while sharing these hilarious moments of imaginative creativity. Later, in a Father's Day note, my daughter wrote when she was nineteen, she recounted these precious moments, documenting them as freshly as if they were occurring that very day instead of many years before.

Taking delight in the experience of living is a trait I witnessed in my mother during my own childhood. She used to say, "Enjoy the good things of life, and share them with others." People loved being in her presence, partly because she relished whatever she was doing, whether savoring a tasty picnic with her children or dropping by to visit a friend, strolling leisurely through the park full of blossoming trees, or sitting down with loved ones at the dinner table with lively conversation and interesting stories of our day. If we set aside time to play and just enjoy our lives, we can relish our connections with others even more.

Entering the Portal of Love

Unfortunately, it took a traumatic event of a heart attack to make me realize the importance of love. I hope you will not have to experience a traumatic event to realize how very important it is to make a conscious choice to enter the portal of love as often as possible. I hope you can learn from my experiences. Although I was raised with love and expressed love, it was after I faced and felt the fragility of life that I wanted and needed to share what I have learned. I realized that I needed to be more loving more often in my everyday life.

In our everyday lives, we can each make this conscious choice to enter the portal of love at any time. We can make this conscious choice whenever we have a relationship challenge. We can imagine the image of LGGC model and set our intention on being drawn into the portal of love. Inside the portal, we can commune with the essence of unconditional love and allow it to permeate every cell in our bodies. When we do this, we will begin to attract more love into our lives. We will have more love to give.

Daily Expressing Love

When we have love to give, we can express it with respect, kind words, and actions, even when the conditions or circumstances don't seem to warrant loving-kindness. To foster love, we have to be honest in little and big matters. To demonstrate love, we can give our undivided attention whether we are at work or at home. Just silently listening and being present can be a loving gesture.

Some ways to consciously express love on a daily basis are to: treat the ones you love like every day is Valentine's Day; e-mail verses or quotes that show love; bake heart-shaped cookies; leave heart-shaped notes in inconspicuous places; send flowers "just because"; be thoughtfully generous with gifts; offer acts of kindness to make someone's life less stressful; and make time to plan events that are mutually enjoyed.

Never forget that love can be applied to any problem. Since this life is short, savor moments by being fun-loving and relishing connections with others. Each day, make a conscious choice to enter the portal of love, and express love to yourself and others.

Key Ideas to Remember about Love

- **Love**
  Love in the LGGC (legacy) model is the first and most complex principle. However, we can access the love portal and any of the others at any time.

- **Love As A Virtue**
  To experience love that is enduring and steady under all circumstances, we must think of it as a principle rather than an emotion. Essentially this kind of love is based on the spiritual principle of the oneness of all life. On this basis, our commitment is to respect the oneness of all people, regardless of whether we like how they think or act.

- **Unconditional Love**
  Rarely do others meet up to our expectations or to the conditions we think we need for our happiness. Genuine love is expressed as well-wishing and goodwill under all circumstances and conditions.

- **Self-Love and—Respect**
  We must first love and respect ourselves before we can truly give love and respect to our neighbors.

- **Loving-Kindness**
  Treating ourselves and others with loving-kindness starts with speaking gently and politely to communicate respect.

- **Honesty**
  Honoring our relationships requires us to be honest with others in a kindly and encouraging way.

- **Balancing Love Relationships and Work**
  We may be physically present without being emotionally or mentally present. What we're aiming for in the portal of love is a sense of being fully present, listening, responding, paying attention, enjoying each other's presence, and conveying positive regard to others, whether at home or at work.

- **Being Truly Present**
  We have the opportunity in each moment to be truly present.

- **Patient Love**
  An important part of positive relationships is spending high-quality time with our loved ones, being emotionally present, listening carefully, responding patiently, paying attention, and truly appreciating their company in the present moment.

- **Love Requires a Heart Connection**
  Keeping an open heart connection is required to truly love. Meditating to discover if we are closing anyone out of our hearts can be helpful to remove blocks from forming a heart connection.

- **Love Requires Action**
  Let us clearly express our love while the other person is still alive and not wait to express our thoughts to their families after he or she is gone.

- **Water as a Symbol of Love**
  Water, like our love, is solvent and carries messages.

- **Relishing Our Connection**
  Let us relish our connection with ourselves and our loved ones and savor each precious moment we share as though it were the last.

- **Entering the Portal of Love**
  We can each make this conscious choice to enter the portal of love at any time.

- **Daily Expressing Love**
  To demonstrate love, we can give our undivided attention when we are with others. We can express love in kind words, honesty, support, problem solving, or even play.

CHAPTER 2

Generosity

Do all the good you can,
By all the means you can,
In all the ways you can,
In all the places you can,
At all the times you can,
To all the people you can,
As long as you can!
—*John Wesley*

Be a lamp, or a lifeboat, or a ladder. Help
someone's soul heal.
—*Rumi*

Generosity

GENEROSITY IS THE SECOND PORTAL in the LGGC (legacy) model. About generosity, Ralph Waldo Emerson said, "Be an opener of doors for such as come after thee." We choose to enter the door or the portal of generosity in the LGGC model when we choose to open doors for others. Many cultures consider generosity a desirous trait. As a result, various dictionaries and wisdom traditions define generosity as:

The habit of giving freely from the heart (e.g., time, skills, attention, material goods) without expecting reciprocation, acknowledgment, or gratitude.

Pure intention of looking out for society's common good.

The antidote for the poison of greed (Buddhism).

The practical outcome of empathy.

The virtue of *caritas*—the Latin term for charity, love, agape, unlimited loving-kindness toward all others—which resides in the will rather than in the emotions (Christianity).

The derivation of the word *generous* involves the concept of nobility, either by birth or by cultivation of one's character. Over the last five centuries, generosity developed from being primarily the description of an ascribed status pertaining to the elite nobility to being an achieved mark of admirable personal quality and action capable of being exercised by any person.

Generosity as a Virtue

Paul's first letter to the Corinthians (13:13) is focused on the virtue of charity or generosity of the *heart in one's character.*

"Though I speak with the tongues of men and of angels, and have not charity, I become as sounding brass, or a tinkling cymbal. And though I have the gift of prophecy, and understand all mysteries, and all knowledge; and though I have all faith, so that I could move mountains, and have not charity, I am nothing. And though I bestow all my goods to feed the poor, and though I give my body to be burned, and have not charity, it profits me nothing. Charity is long suffering and is kind; charity envies not. Charity does not vaunt itself, is not puffed up, does not behave unseemly, seeks not her own, is not easily provoked, and thinks no evil; Charity rejoices not in iniquity, but rejoices in the truth. Charity bears all things, believes all things, hopes all things, and endures all things. Charity never fails: but where there are prophecies, they shall fail; where there are tongues, they shall cease; where there is knowledge, it shall vanish away. And now abide in faith, hope, charity—these three; but the greatest of these is charity."

Generosity Requires Humility

Giving from the heart also goes hand-in-hand with humility. Puffing up our own image and acting out of self-serving ambition at the expense of others are the marks of egoistic pride, which are likely to diminish any relationship. In *The Teachings of Don Juan* by Carlos Castaneda, the wise Yaqui mentor says we should always choose a path from the heart.

If we choose a path out of greed or ambition, we will live to regret that choice. When we choose to act out of authentic generosity and humility, we are looking for ways to serve rather than boost our own authority or power. Philippines 2:3 in The Bible states "Do nothing from selfish ambition or conceit, but in humility count others more significant than yourselves."

Considering others who are significant to us, we want to give to them and serve them. Once a Buddhist student at the university told me that in his family upbringing, he was taught the highest form of worship is service to others. Since then, I have come to know that pure generosity in the form of humble service is one of the most basic ethical tenets not only in Buddhism but also in many other wisdom traditions. My father used to say that the tree that's bent over is the one that bears the most fruit. I have found that giving generously and serving others flow from a feeling of humility deep within my heart.

The ancient law of circulation requires that we give others whatever we wish to have for ourselves. If we want love, then we must give love; if we want peace, then we must give peace; if we want prosperity, then we must give prosperity to help others gain prosperity. Giving generously is a by-product of the profound strength of character that comes from genuine humility.

When we have humility, we are willing to take a look at our own thoughts, motivation, and actions and are willing to learn and grow from our observations. We can also humbly learn from the criticism of others. If criticism is warranted, we can

25

use the points of criticism as pathways to learning. By learning from criticism, we are humbly accepting the help of others, even when it is offered in an irritating or painful form.

Unconditional Generosity

True generosity is unconditional. Unconditional generosity is giving without anticipation of any kind of reciprocation, repayment, or even a thank you. At different times in our lives, we give for a variety of reasons. To ascertain whether our giving or the giving of others is truly generous, we need to look at the intentions of the heart. The question is not did we give, but "Did we give generously?"

For example, two movie stars, who will remain anonymous, chose to give time and talent in support of a fundraiser for cancer research. One star gave talent because national media coverage would result in exposure to millions of television viewers. The gift of time and talent was simply in exchange for gaining more fame. That act is not giving from the heart in the spirit of generosity but is striking a good bargain or trading. However, the second movie star had a grandmother who died from cancer and has been donating funds to cancer research for twenty-three years. Since the second movie star gave out of a heartfelt gesture, then the giving was authentically generous.

Conversely, companies that offer beneficial goods and services may potentially be taken over by profit motives. The generosity motive begins to be deflected, greed may set in, and services may be refused if they are not obviously profitable. Cheating and misrepresentation may occur behind closed doors. Greed that replaces generosity as the primary motive has sparked a downward trend in some of the greatest companies. These kinds of disasters occur not only at the company level but at the individual, community, national, and global levels as well, leading to economic crises of vast proportions—all ignited when generosity dies and greed arises. However, when a true desire to serve remains as the impetus for working, we can learn and even expand our scope with generosity.

When we give, are we giving generously? Are we thinking that we are being generous when we are actually setting conditions to ensure we will benefit from our giving?

Conditional Giving

Setting conditions before giving to others may be necessary or wise. For example, if we agree to allow a teenager driver who just obtained a driver's license to take the family car for the first time, we may need to establish conditions for our giving. Of course, in this case, we need to set limits, establish a mutual agreement, and get a promise from the recipient—*I'll let you have the keys as long as you return at such and such time and only do so and so.* These conditional agreements are common. Yet at times these agreements can be scary or create anxiety when they require a level of profound trust before the agreement or trade is even made.

What often happens in these types of conditional agreements is if the other person doesn't live up to his/her promised part of the bargain, we may react in anger, sadness, accusation, or blame. The outcome of this type of agreement could then potentially lead to disappointment for both parties.

Many people set conditions and expectations, issue demands, make bargains, or say, *I'll care about you or give to you only if you do what I'm expecting.* We may withhold our affection, criticize, point at each other with blame, seek revenge, and fester in our hearts when we feel hurt, enraged, and ashamed. We may lose sleep or obsess over unhealthy thoughts.

On the other hand, if we give freely with no conditions set for the giving, then no matter what the outcome, we know the giving was from our free volition and choice. If the gift that was freely given has a negative outcome, we are much less likely to erupt in negative emotions (e.g., anger, frustration, sadness, horror). Rather, we are more likely to respond from one of the other three portals (love, gratitude, or compassion) concerning the outcome. In this scenario, by responding with love, gratitude, or compassion, we are opening the opportunity to expand life rather than contract it.

Finding Generosity in Strained Relationships

What are some examples of a lack of generosity during a difficult relationship? Perhaps we have been disappointed that someone didn't meet up to our standards, needs, wants, and expectations. We may have yielded to the pressure or demands of others and such giving was done not out of pure heart or unconditionally. Maybe we acted out of fear or disapproval or our own actions based upon a false definition of generosity. When we give someone something based on fear, guilt, or avoidance of pressure, ironically our giving has a life-constricting effect, and such giving can only harm the relationship. In fact, giving based on a negative emotion comes at a negative cost. To avoid negative consequences, we want to remember that generosity is giving freely from the heart. Unconditional love is the primary wellspring of generosity in the LGGC (legacy) model. Anything given not from the heart in a relationship is most likely to result into disappointment, anger, hatred, duress, revenge, abuse, codependency, imbalance, and other forms of not truly loving.

If we detect anything other than genuine generosity in our motivations, actions, or words, then we are wise to seek deeper understanding. The solution will probably come from learning how to give purely and freely while honoring ourselves and others rather than issuing or yielding to demands. A higher degree of self-examination and mindfulness may lead to an uncomfortable change in a relationship. Such examination nevertheless offers a greater chance for emotional healing to take place through forgiveness, humility, and honesty. Emotional healing nurtures and sustains both our relationships and our own self-development.

Generosity can be activated in any context—in our personal domain, the community, the nation, or the world.

Personal Generosity

Even while at home, a knock at the door can provide an opportunity to convey personal generosity and to expand life in unexpected ways. For example, I know a family in Colombia who never locked their doors, even during the worst times of the drug cartel wars in that country. One evening, Mrs. Salazar answered the rapping on the front door, only to find one of her son's former friends. The young man standing there looked disheveled, dirty, and distraught as he asked Mrs. Salazar for some food. She invited him in, prepared a nutritious dinner, and sat with him at the table as he gobbled it down. Afterward she invited him to take a warm shower and sleep in the guest bedroom for the night. In the morning, she gave him some clean clothes that had belonged to her son, who died at the age of forty. The young man thanked her and left feeling refreshed, relaxed, and genuinely cared for.

About a year passed before she spoke with him again. She ran into him waiting in line for a bus to arrive. He was dressed nicely in a suit and tie, neatly groomed, and cleanly shaven. He looked her straight in the eye and said, "Thank you, Mrs. Salazar, for what you did for me that night. You gave me food, warmth, a shower, a comfortable bed to sleep in for the night, and clean clothes. You also respected me and treated me with kindness, without regard to my appearance and situation. In fact, for a long time, I had been addicted to drugs and was crashing at the houses of people I didn't even know, passing out, and feeling lost and alone. Mostly those people resented me and told me never to bother them again, even though they were still willing to take me in for just one night. I remember more than anything their frowning faces and their judgment of me as a despicable human being, but you were different. You simply extended your gracious kindness and gave me what you had without any feeling of blame or loathing. As I left your home the following morning, I knew at that moment I would make definite changes in my life. The nonjudgmental acceptance and kindheartedness of your generosity was a catalyst for me to turn my life around. Thank you from the bottom of my heart!"

Mrs. Salazar passed away a few years later without seeing this man again. She left the invisible touch of her simple acts of kindness shared that evening. Who knows how many lives that man went on to influence in a positive way as a result? By putting her generosity into circulation through him and many others, she left a life-expanding legacy for this world. We can do the same!

There are people like Mrs. Salazar everywhere. In New York City, a cab driver by the name of Mukul Asaduzzaman found a purse left by one of his customers in the backseat of his taxi. Inside the purse was ten thousand dollars in cash! How many people would keep the money for themselves? Not Mukul. He found a name, Felicia Lettieri, and an address in the purse, drove fifty miles out to Long Island, and left a note to her since she was not home ("Don't worry, Felicia . . . I'll keep it safe"), along with his contact information. The seventy-two-year-old Italian tourist had earlier been told by the police that whoever found the money probably would not return it. She was surprised and thrilled that the money she had saved to cover expenses for a family vacation of seven people had been returned.

When a *NY Post* newspaper reporter, Brad Hamilton asked Mukul why he didn't keep the cash for himself, he said simply that when he was five years old, his mother told him to be honest and work hard, and he would prosper. He even refused to accept a sizable reward—a perfect reminder that true generosity of the heart does not seek personal gain for the giving. The only real reward is the feeling of deep contentment that comes from doing what we know to be right.

Community Generosity

An example of a generous person is Sanjit "Bunker" Roy, who founded India's Barefoot College in 1972. His compassion for the people living in impoverished conditions inspired him to raise the quality of life for his people in a way that would foster dignity, self-worth, and sustainable prosperity rather than just providing a handout that could be used up quickly. He created a grassroots socioeconomic organization that recruited villagers (mostly the elderly and women) to the free college for professional training as teachers, midwives, weavers, doctors, nurses, dentists, and solar engineers. These "barefoot professionals" returned to their villages to put their training to practical use by creating self-sustaining and humanitarian projects. Examples of such projects included installing electricity, clean water, and wasteland reclaiming systems; building homes; establishing clinics; and setting up local handicraft factories. The new institutions are owned and managed by the very same village people who are being served by students' offerings.

India's Barefoot College is now functioning nationwide; over the past thirty-nine years, it has recruited and trained more than 3 million villagers. Sanjit Roy was named in 2010 among the "100 Most Influential Personalities in the World" by *Time Magazine*. The awareness and empathy of this one dedicated human being materialized as a project that stands as a vibrant model of generosity in the modern world.

Global Generosity

A huge and unexpected result may materialize from a tiny act of generosity. One afternoon in 2004, Salman Khan, a high-level investment analyst, was asked by a cousin living in a distant US state for help with her math homework. Salman was the right family member to ask. He graduated at the top of his class as a math major from MIT and finished his business degree from Harvard Business School. To help his cousin, Salman answered her questions by posting a series of short tutorials on the Internet. Subsequently, she and several of her friends watched the tutorials and easily mastered the math concepts they formerly didn't grasp.

Gradually, the number of hits on Salman's YouTube tutorials grew exponentially to more than one hundred thousand hits per month. Students have been supplementing their knowledge and understanding with Salman's clear, precise, brief, repeatable, and in-depth explanations. These tutorials form a library of 2,400 videos, 180 practice exercises, and coaching exercises on a wide variety of academic subjects ranging from math to science, humanities, history, finance, banking, and standardized test preparation. What is known as the Khan Academy has already delivered more than 78 million free lessons to people located all over the world via the Internet. Translations have been donated in a variety of languages.

Interestingly enough, Salman Khan didn't dream up this project as a way of making money but simply as a way of helping a family member and her friends understand the concepts in their schoolwork—a perfect illustration of plain generosity that flourishes naturally to fill a need. At first, Salman paid for what little equipment he needed out of his own bank account. Gradually the ten-minute online tutorials became self-supporting via ads that appeared on the screen, from which Salman derived a percentage. He enjoyed the online teaching so much that he decided to resign from his job as an investment analyst. Khan devotes his time to researching new subjects for the expanding repertoire of academic subjects that are being avidly watched by thousands of people worldwide at home, in classrooms, and at community centers in tiny villages.

Recently Bill Gates worked through some of the lessons on the Khan Academy and decided to have his children use them as a basic part of their learning. Subsequently, he gave a $15 million grant to the nonprofit Khan Academy to help support this magnificent educational project that is now available for free to all people who have Internet access. The generosity of people like Salman Khan starts in the purity of heart that takes delight in helping others rather than using others for one's own personal gain.

This example doesn't mean we can't personally gain or earn a good living. Making money is a wonderful thing, especially when we can be of great service to humanity by creating projects that genuinely help people. In turn, we profit from these projects, thereby circulating prosperity through waves of mutual benefit.

Through expanding our generosity, we not only improve our human relationships, but we also nurture and sustain our relationship with Mother Earth and all nature. In 2004, the Nobel Peace Prize was awarded to an East African woman, Wangari Maathai, an environmentalist, feminist, university professor, and human rights activist, for her contribution to sustainable development, democracy, and peace. She founded the Green Belt Movement from a small circle of conservationists by planting seven trees in the Kamukunji Park on the outskirts of Nairobi. She encouraged the women of Kenya to search in the forests near their homes for seeds of trees native to their area to plant. Then Wangari Maathai told these women to transplant them elsewhere and start tree nurseries. This extraordinary woman, who was eventually elected to the parliament and served as assistant minister of environment and nature, heightened ecological awareness in Kenya and around the globe. By the time she died at the age of seventy-one, more than 45 million trees had been planted in Africa, and more than nine hundred thousand women had established tree nurseries to reverse the damaging effects of deforestation throughout the country. This one woman's courage, insight, caring, and provision of time and talent exemplify the goodness that is cultivated through dedication and tireless giving.

Earth's Generosity

The generosity of environmentalists such as Wangari reflects the generosity of the earth itself. The generosity of the earth is extreme. We can take a tiny seed and cast it aside onto the dirt beneath our feet. Nature goes quietly to work on the little seed right away with moisture and nutrients in the rain and soil. Pretty soon, the seed will begin to unfold the genetic material inherent within its shell. The sprouts root, and its tendrils grow deeper into the earth. Then we see miniature buds, and finally a sturdy, flourishing plant in full bloom. Even if we uproot the plant, grind it down, and throw it away, the cycle continues. The pulverized plant fertilizes the soil, helps seeds take root, grow, and even begin to take over the natural environment wherever they happen to flourish. By growing, even under the harshest conditions, the plants keep on giving to others, and bounty is a beautiful example of unconditional generosity.

In contrast, conditional giving causes imbalance. We will do well to emulate nature and choose to feel and act with unconditional regard and respect, which results in generosity of spirit in all our dealings with others and with nature.

How do we get in tune with the inner workings of nature as "evolved" creatures that possess awareness and volition? We can use that same volition to choose understanding of the bigger picture. As spiritual centers of the universal creative intelligence and generosity, we can develop habits and attitudes that will allow us to act from our natural state of love. We can glean insight into the beauty and gentle power of natural generosity through developing the practice of meditation, praying, listening to our inner voice of intuition, learning from our experiences and the expertise of others, and/or acting on our generous impulses. From these practices, we may become more patient and empathic with the life all around us, such as our fellow human beings, animals, plants, rocks, rivers, and air. We may restore balance in all our relationships and strengthen our sense of pleasure and joy in this life. It's not too late.

Entering the Portal of Generosity

It is never too late to enter the portal of generosity. We can make a conscious choice to visualize the LGGC (legacy) model and focus our intention on entering the portal of generosity. We can think about generous people we have known in our lives and visualize the specific things they did to demonstrate generosity. We can then decide how we want to demonstrate generosity ourselves. Of course, we can give our financial resources, but we can also give our precious, limited time and show we are truly interested in others.

Daily Expressing Generosity

We can learn to express generosity by observing others around us who naturally express this trait. For example, when I was at Macy's buying some chocolates for my doctor's office staff, a sales clerk generously shared a smile and a profound statement with me: "Money spent on others is money well spent."

In our daily lives, there are many opportunities for each of us to enter the portal of generosity and then genuinely express it. We can offer a smile, help someone with shelter, teach what others need to know, lend a helping hand, encourage with our words, listen, send thank-you notes, give a gift card, share coupons, take a meal to a service provider, and offer to sit with someone.

Other ways to daily express generosity include: giving to charity, sharing random acts of kindness, tipping well, and giving people more than they expect. We can act on a generous impulse that comes to mind. Whatever we do may seem insignificant, but it is important that we take generous action.

Key Ideas to Remember About Generosity

- **Generosity**
  We choose to enter the door or the portal of Generosity in the LGGC model when we choose to open doors for others.

- **Generosity as Virtue**
  The virtue of generosity involves giving unselfishly to help others without expecting anything in return, not even acknowledgment or appreciation.

- **Generosity Requires Humility**
  A subtle aspect of generosity is staying humble, which involves serving others unselfishly, being willing to accept help even from the criticism of others, taking opportunities to grow and learn, and remaining unattached to the outward symbols of success.

- **Unconditional Generosity**
  Unconditional generosity is giving without anticipation of any kind of reciprocation, repayment, or even thank you.

- **Conditional Giving**
  Conditional giving happens when we set conditions and expectations, issue demands, make bargains, or say, "I'll care about you or give to you only if you act to achieve the outcome that I wish."

- **Personal Generosity**
  In acts of personal generosity (e.g., giving food, shelter), the only real reward is the sense of deep contentment that comes from doing what we know is right.

- **Finding Generosity during Relationship Difficulties**
  Giving based on a negative emotion comes at a negative cost. To avoid negative consequences, we want to remember that generosity is giving freely from the heart.

- **Community Generosity**
  We can transform one individual's generosity into a valuable project that serves the entire community or nation, such as the Barefoot College that fosters sustainable prosperity and beneficial grassroots industries throughout India.

- **Global Generosity**
  The pure generosity of a single person can become globally beneficial, as in the free Internet tutorials of Khan Academy or the Green Belt Movement founded by one courageous woman from Kenya.

- **Earth's Generosity**
  We see the earth's generosity in the continuous growth of plant life even under the harshest conditions.

- **Entering the Portal of Generosity**
  We can think about generous people we have known in our lives and visualize the specific things they did to

demonstrate generosity. We can then decide how we want to demonstrate generosity ourselves.

- **Daily Expressing Generosity**
  We can offer a smile, teach what others need to know, lend a helping hand, encourage with our words, listen, give our time, send thank-you notes, give a gift card, share coupons, and call and offer to sit with someone at a shelter, mission, hospice, or nursing home.

CHAPTER 3

Gratitude

He is a wise man who does not grieve
for the things which he has not, but rejoices
for those which he has.
—Epictetus

Gratitude

CICERO, IN ANCIENT ROMAN TIMES, believed that gratitude was the "parent of all the other virtues." Gratitude is the feeling and attitude of appreciation for the benefits we have received or expect to receive. Gratitude is often the easiest portal for many of us to enter in the LGGC model, even when the other three portals appear to be blocked or are just too challenging to enter in the moment. After we begin to feel grateful, little by little, we can usually feel more open to love, generosity, or compassion.

It's naturally easy to be grateful for positive and pleasant experiences and gifts. However, we are wise to be grateful for even those events that we experience as difficult or negative. We can develop a habit of feeling grateful in general, of consciously looking for or having faith there is a benefit in every situation. In fact, what appears to be bad is actually goodness or gratitude opportunities waiting to be discovered.

Gratitude as a Virtue

Gratitude is regarded as a virtue that shapes emotions, thoughts, and actions. According to A. M. Wood and other researchers at the University of Manchester, grateful people are happier, less depressed, less stressed, and more satisfied with their lives and social relationships. Grateful people also have higher levels of control of their environments, personal growth, purpose in life, and self-acceptance. They have more positive ways of coping with the difficulties they experience in life. (Wood & Maltby 2008).

Such people are more likely to seek support, reinterpret and grow from the experience, and spend more time planning how to deal with the problem. Grateful people also have less negative coping strategies because they are less likely to try to avoid the problem, deny there is a problem, blame themselves, or cope through substance use. They sleep better, and this seems to be because they think fewer negative and more positive thoughts just before going to sleep. Gratitude is one of the strongest links with good mental health of any character trait. Those who approach life with a sense of gratitude make it a point to be aware of what's wonderful and successful in their lives and share their gratitude with others.

Unconditional Gratitude

Similar to the other LGGC principles, authentic gratitude is unconditional. Indebtedness or obligation to repay a giver, in contrast, is conditional. Feeling indebted may motivate the recipient to avoid the person who gave help. This happens especially if s/he is unable to repay the debt. This avoidance can harm the relationship by bringing greater distance or disconnection between those involved. On the contrary, feeling gratitude often motivates the recipient to become closer to the giver since no obligation was attached to the gift in the first place.

Freely expressed gratitude is akin to unconditional giving in that gratitude usually improves our relationships because it is proffered unconditionally, with no thought of receiving appreciation in return.

Gratitude Impacts Well-Being and Disposition

Gratitude, it turns out, makes us happier and healthier. In a study on gratitude, conducted by Robert A. Emmons, PhD, at the University of California at Davis and his colleague Mike McCullough at the University of Miami, randomly assigned participants, who were given one of three tasks. Each week, participants kept a short journal. One group briefly described five things they were grateful for that had occurred in the past week, another five recorded daily hassles from the previous week that displeased them, and the neutral group was asked to list five events or circumstances that affected them, but they were not told whether to focus on the positive or on the negative. Ten weeks later, participants in the gratitude group felt better about their lives as a whole and were a full 25 percent happier than the hassled group. They reported fewer health complaints and exercised an average of 1.5 hours more. (Emmons, R.A. & M. E. McCullough 2003).

Gratitude not only improves health and happiness, but in additional research Dr. Prof. Robert Emmons at the University of California, Davis focused on the role of gratitude in increasing our levels of well-being throughout our personal and social lives. The following are some of Dr. Emmons's findings that demonstrate a significant link between gratitude and well-being.

- Participants who kept gratitude lists for two months were more likely to have made progress toward important personal goals (academic, interpersonal, and health based) compared to subjects in the other experimental conditions.
- A daily gratitude intervention (self-guided exercises) with young adults resulted in higher reported levels of the positive states of alertness, enthusiasm,

determination, attentiveness, and energy compared to groups with a focus on hassles or a downward social comparison (ways in which participants thought they were better off than others). No differences in levels of unpleasant emotions were reported in the three groups.

- Participants in the group expressing daily gratitude were more likely to report helping someone with a personal problem or offering emotional support relative to groups with a focus on hassles or social comparison.

Emmons and colleagues have also devised scales to measure grateful disposition:

- Well-being: Grateful people report higher levels of positive emotions, life satisfaction, vitality, and optimism and lower levels of depression and stress. The disposition toward gratitude appears to enhance pleasant-feeling states more than it diminishes unpleasant emotions. Grateful people do not deny or ignore the negative aspects of life.
- Caring behavior: People with a strong disposition toward gratitude have the capacity to be empathetic. They are rated as more generous and more helpful by people in their social networks (McCullough, Emmons, & Tsang, 2002).
- Spirituality: Those who regularly attend religious services and engage in religious activities, such as prayer or reading religious material, are more likely

to be grateful than nonreligious people. Grateful people are more likely to acknowledge a belief in the interconnectedness of all life and a commitment to and responsibility to others compared to people who do not consciously pick gratitude. Gratitude does not require religious faith, but faith enhances the ability to be grateful.

- Materialism: Grateful individuals place less importance on material goods; they are less likely to judge their own and others' success in terms of possessions accumulated. Grateful people are less envious of others and are more likely to share their possessions with others relative to less-grateful persons.

Having a disposition of gratitude engenders other virtues—humility, compassion, wisdom, joy, integrity, and trust. Feeling grateful and expressing our gratitude is not just an emotional response to events or situations. Being grateful is truly a committed choice we make in any given context to experience greater wellness and vitality in our lives.

Accepting Oneself and Others

Grateful people are those who are willing to take a look at themselves. The law of reflection indicates that whatever disturbs us in others is a reflection of some hidden aspect of ourselves that's yearning for our attention and self-acceptance. Think of something/someone/some situation that causes anger, hurt, or pain.

- Ask, how must that person be feeling inside? What subconscious memories are probably being triggered and running rampant in him/her? What role is s/he playing under the influence of these controlling subconscious memories? What kind of events or situations in early childhood most likely planted these subconscious memories?

- Ask, what part of me feels similar to the other person? What actions, roles, or conflicts are similar to the other person's?

- Go slowly; take time to work through this process that may bring up tears or painful images. Once we have hit upon an insight into our own traits or damaging behaviors, we must take time to talk to the hidden part of us that has come to the surface of our conscious mind.

- As we allow ourselves to feel kind and loving toward that painful part from past memories, feel the freedom that comes from loving all of us, including this part, not just the approved and pretty parts of our exterior character and personality. As we accept this part of our whole human experience, we will lessen the pressure of these rampaging subconscious memories. We will experience the peaceful feeling of caring for ourselves wholly and unconditionally.

The beauty of self-acceptance and self-forgiveness as the basis of loving and forgiving others is that such acceptance keeps us from harming ourselves and others. When we are precious to ourselves, our self-respect does not allow us to harm any other being. Being grateful for ourselves, valuing who we are—even with all our mistakes and flaws—establishes the foundation upon which we can be grateful for others. One way we can practice being grateful for ourselves is to look at the mirror when brushing our teeth and think about something we have done well recently or something we like about ourselves.

Reveling in the Ordinary

Being grateful for the ordinary things and events in our daily lives contributes in a profound and practical way to our well-being and happiness. If we rush through our day's activities without paying attention to what we're doing or feeling thankful for what's in front of us, we are going through our events without really experiencing them. This state of mindlessness is a way of being numb or cut off from the present moment.

To the contrary, feeling grateful for what's in our experience is loving life. Loving life fills our heart with song and good cheer, which we may then radiate outward and share with others. I was recently talking about LGGC to a mother of a once-beautiful, delightful daughter who a methamphetamine addict was trying unsuccessfully to recover. One morning, the mother was so enraged over the recent hysterical behavior of her daughter that she really could not feel love, compassion, or generosity at all. The mother stood in her kitchen feeling angry, confused, and afraid, and she remembered our conversation. *If I can't feel loving right now, maybe I can at least feel grateful,* she thought. The damaged condition of their current relationship was too overwhelming for anything like unconditional appreciation to emerge. No matter how much she may have liked to, she really couldn't feel grateful for anything about her daughter at that moment.

She closed her eyes in frustration and hopelessness, sensing that she needed to become calm to make it through the morning with sanity. *When I open my eyes, I will see something to be genuinely grateful for,* she thought. After a few moments of listening to herself breathing, she slowly opened her eyes, only to find that she was looking directly at the white refrigerator across the room. A feeling of humor, release, and relief spread throughout her body as she allowed herself to feel grateful for that old refrigerator. The refrigerator was humming away, working diligently on her behalf to keep the family's perishables fresh so she could make a nutritious breakfast for the three grandsons in her foster care.

That plain feeling of thankfulness for an ordinary refrigerator broke the spell of rage and ushered in a measure of peace and joy, allowing her to start her day in a loving mode. After breakfast, the two-year-old said, "Thanks, Jammy—that was tasty!" His sweet words innocently reflected the very attitude and feeling of gratitude she had been able to attain only through intentional and conscious effort. When she told me about this episode, I suddenly felt even more grateful for my own refrigerator and the food inside it.

We should revel in the ordinary. If we are folding the laundry, for instance, then we can be grateful and happy for the clean laundry, the fresh scent of the clean clothes, the washer and dryer, the capacity to do this labor, the plumbing that brings running water, and the softened textures of the clean laundry.

Being grateful for what is already in our lives allows us to use wisely what we have in our ordinary experience. Jessica Cox is a twenty-eight-year-old woman who was born without arms. Fitted for prosthetic limbs in her childhood, she tried to adapt to them but found them bulky and irritating. Finally, at the age of fourteen she decided that, rather than trying to be like everyone else with arms and hands, she would learn how to use what she already had—her legs and feet. "Instead of investing so much time in being normal," she said, "I realized it was more important to celebrate my differences."

Tossing her prosthetic arms into the back of the closet, Jessica learned with persistence how to do just about everything with her feet and toes that most people do with their hands and fingers. She soon learned how to drive a car and afterward received her driver's license. In 2008, she earned her sport pilot's license and now flies her own Ercoupe plane, using one foot to manage the control panel and the other to deftly guide the steering column. Besides being the first person in the world licensed to fly a plane with only one's feet, Jessica regularly swims and walks briskly to keep fit and flexible. She brushes her teeth, applies cosmetics, takes out contact lenses, writes, unwraps packages, and does most other tasks with her feet and toes. She has two black belts in Tae Kwon Do as well as a college degree in psychology. She maintains an active motivational speaking career that focuses on inspiring others to appreciate and use what they already have in their daily lives. By being grateful for what she did have—her legs and feet—and developing the skills to use them effectively, Jessica turned what was ordinary in her life into extraordinary achievement.

Making gratitude a habit of our daily lives is a worthy goal, not something we have to force ourselves to feel with strenuous effort. Like Jessica, with clear intention, commitment, mindfulness, and steady practice amid the setbacks, we begin to experience a sense of appreciation more and more often until finally we develop the habit of being thankful nearly every step of the way. Pretty soon we'll be telling others how much we appreciate them and celebrating life moment by moment.

Living in the Present Moment

Cultivating a disposition and habit of gratitude through these and other daily practices helps us to experience life with greater mindfulness in each passing moment. Every time we think, *'I should have, could have, or would have'* we are diminishing the creative power of our present moment as well as the joy of the subsequent moments. No two moments are ever the same. Everything changes, so we do not want to take any unique moment for granted, nor do we want to deny its creative power by ignoring the moment. Cherishing this moment opens the way to perceiving increased blessings now and in the next moment.

What does it mean to live in the present moment? One part of the answer to that question is to seek guidance from the universal creative intelligence and wisdom nestled in our own subconscious minds. To bring to our conscious awareness universal intelligence, we choose to listen to the still, small voice within and trust its ever-changing guidance. The inner wisdom and intuitive insight is always fresh and appropriate for any particular situation. A similar situation in the future will be guided differently; no two bits of advice from the inner voice are identical. Following the sacred inner guidance from universal creative intelligence provides a foundation for living in freedom and courage during each unique moment of our lives. When we act according to our interior spiritual wisdom, we know we are doing the right thing for any particular occasion. If we ignore or silence the intuitive voice within, we will often live to regret that choice. At best, some goodness is delayed and frustration sets in. At worst, prolonged regret from dismissing our inner voice dampens us, flavoring our life experience with sorrow and emptiness.

Create Your Legacy

Of course, we want to honor and learn from our past experiences to live wisely and renewed in the present moment. Those who cannot remember the past often repeat it. The important thing is to put into practice what we have learned by not repeating the same old patterns of thinking and acting that have led to unhappy outcomes in the past. I often hear people paraphrasing the ancient Chinese proverb, "The definition of insanity is doing the same thing over and over again, yet expecting different results." Learning from our past experience is a way of releasing the hold of the past over us emotionally—the hold of regret, disapproval, guilt, and shame. Rather than getting caught in mourning our past choices and situations, we pay attention to the significance of these choices and then apply new understanding to our current choices and possibilities. To maintain a healthy body and mind we need to put an end to mourning about the past, worrying about the future, or anticipating trouble; instead we must learn to live in the present moment earnestly.

We are wise to be awake and vigilant to the inner voice of guidance and counsel in each present moment. The time to awaken is now! Being grateful is certainly a vital part of being awake, feeling alive, and having fun. Truly, a grateful heart makes each passing moment precious, valuable, and full. It is vital for us to express what is deep in our heart without hesitation and delay. We can't take our own health or life for granted, nor that of our friends or loved ones. Nothing in the realm of form is permanent, and so we are wise to cherish each opportunity and express our gratitude as it arises.

Entering the Portal of Gratitude

At first we may need a great deal of determination to remain devoted to deliberately looking for things to be grateful for every day, but it is an important spiritual practice well worth cultivating. Gratitude opens the door that allows us to hear our inner insight, which grants us our freedom. To be grateful for something, we must be grateful for what we have already received! Gratitude opens doors that do not otherwise open. This is a spiritual fact.

As a child, I was fortunate to be immersed in a family in which the habit of gratitude was the norm because my parents daily showed gratitude in deed and shared it in word. Even when there was disappointment, concern, or loss, they still had a deep appreciation for what we had: our friends, family, and other people and for life itself. Later, as I matured, I witnessed perspectives in other families, and I gradually began to notice the radical difference that being genuinely grateful makes in life. I could see that gratitude was more than just maintaining a polite and socially cohesive demeanor toward others. I learned that gratitude is profound because it shifts one's thoughts, feelings, and perceptions from negative to positive.

In an intense or difficult relationship, we may resist expressing gratitude even if we feel it. We can easily fall into the habit of not even saying "Thank you" or "You're welcome" as we normally do in other relationships that are less strained. Yet, ironically, one effective way to break through the barrier of anger and hurt is to start expressing our appreciation. The other person in a strained relationship may be surprised to hear us say, "I really appreciate that you helped me yesterday afternoon at the office party" or "Thanks for helping me walk the dogs." The expression of appreciation has to be sincere and specific to pierce the shell of defense that has built up over time. With persistence built from deliberately watching for things to appreciate, we can witness these seemingly small expressions of gratitude begin to soften the relationship and gradually bring greater peace and harmony.

Practices for Cultivating Gratitude

Gratitude Inventory

Baruch Spinoza, seventeenth-century philosopher, suggested that we often ask ourselves the following questions to find more meaning and joy in our lives:

1. Who or what inspired me today?
2. What brought me happiness today?
3. What brought me comfort and deep peace today?

Other writers also stress the importance of cultivating the outlook and habit of thankfulness by keeping a gratitude list or gratitude journal. For example, John Randolph Price emphasizes in his, *The Abundance Book* the power of making a list every single day for which we are grateful. He says if you can't think of anything right away, just look around you in the room, and surely you'll see something you appreciate, like your comfortable chair or a beautiful painting on the wall. On days when you don't take the time to jot down the list on paper, at least go through a list in your mind, perhaps as you are driving somewhere or waiting for an appointment. Keep thinking of or stating aloud one thing after another that you're really grateful for until you reach your destination or the appointment begins. (Price 1997).

On one occasion, I was sitting at the car dealership waiting for my car to be repaired and had nothing with me to read and no calls to make. Just for fun, I decided to use that free time to make a list of what I appreciated in life. On my list were material things, relationships, people, nature, and situations that were present in my life at the time; some were events planned for the future, and others were from the past.

At the very top of the list was an event that occurred when I was eight years old. As my cousin and I were returning home from soccer practice one afternoon, we started running to see who was faster. Just on the other side of the soccer field was a busy street. My cousin was ahead of me, and as we dashed into the street, I looked both ways and saw no traffic. All of a sudden, my cousin turned around and started running back toward the soccer field. I thought that was strange, but I kept running forward, determined to win the competition. The next thing I knew, I was lying in the street, looking up into the bottom of a car. I'll never forget seeing the huge engine and feeling its heat just above me as the car ran over my body and kept going. I was knocked unconscious. The next day I woke up in the hospital and saw the school principal standing near my mother at the foot of the bed. *I must be in bad trouble*, was all I could think with the two of them there. As my eyes opened, my mother fell on me, weeping for joy that I was alive! I had survived being run over with no disabilities or lasting effects. This survival is something to be grateful for! All of us have had close calls, which are gratitude opportunities.

Lately I have started the practice of naming at least three things I'm truly grateful for upon awakening each morning. I'm finding it's delightful to make a mental inventory of positive items. Indeed, one positive thought leads to another, and it's practically impossible to limit myself to only three things. It's much more fun to start the day in a pleasant state of mind with a feeling of calm in my heart engendered by the gratitude inventory. This sets a positive tone for the day. If I start the day with worry, fear, or resentment attitudes, it builds on itself and generates a day of more of the same. Below are some other interesting ways we can focus on enhancing gratitude.

The OOPS Game!

Whenever we catch ourselves being critical of anything or anyone, we can just say aloud "OOPS!" (Out of Principle, Sweetheart!). Then quickly think of something you're grateful for instead, either related to the scenario or not.

A perfect opportunity, for example, might be when we catch ourselves criticizing a driver who has suddenly changed lanes without signaling, almost colliding with a car already in that lane. We would usually think, *What an idiot that driver was!* As soon as we hear ourselves condemning the driver, we can quickly say out loud, "OOPS!" followed by, "I'm very grateful that I have a car with good brakes." When we make a habit of playing the OOPS game, we become increasingly aware of the quality of our passing thoughts and thus gradually become more grateful, happy, and calm instead of harsh, rigid, angry, judgmental, and tense. Playing the OOPS game throughout the day in the spirit of playfulness and fun can increase our level of happiness with very little effort.

Mentor List

Another version of the gratitude inventory is the mentor list. Once in a while, we can think of a professor, teacher, colleague, friend's parent, or anyone else who has had a beneficial effect on our lives.

Rather than just letting these images float by almost unnoticed, I decided to create a Microsoft Excel spreadsheet. I made columns to capture the person's name, role, what he or she did specifically to help me, what happened as a result of his or her help, and what might have happened differently in my life had that person not mentored me. Not only does this spreadsheet elevate my own sense of gratitude, but it also helps me look for ways in which I may serve as a mentor or positive role model in someone else's life. Examination of the spreadsheet expands my feeling of zest and dedication to deliberately look out for ways to be a beneficial presence. Sir Isaac Newton recommended being appreciative of those who have opened the way for us. He said that his discoveries were possible only because he was able to stand on the shoulders of the giants who had gone before him. In a way, our mentors are our giants. They have opened the way by showing they have faith in us to use our talents for spreading greater goodness in life.

Gratitude Notes

I found a group of people online who created Life University-Happy L.I.F.E in focus offering the public some of the existing research in positive psychology and simple, practical applications that may help us increase the positivity in our lives. This experiment in positive thinking is based on the following six principles:

- Exercise
- Gratitudes
- Journaling
- Meditation
- The Life In Focus Experiment
- Written Thank-You's

One of the principles I found to be most valuable is their suggestion of keeping a 'gratitude list, journaling, and paying 'gratitude visits' to people who have supported us, and remain our loyal friends. Additionally, we are to take the time to write 'gratitude notes/letters' thanking our family, friends, and acquaintances who remain positively connected with us, thus enhancing our lives.

Typically in the past, before my heart attack, I might have thought of someone I was grateful for but then decided it might be inappropriate to send a note or call. After the health crisis, I was no longer inclined to hold back the expression of my appreciation. Indeed, I felt such actions were important to do. According to research, I was actually improving my own health by feeling and sharing my grateful thoughts with those people. Now I intend to make this kind of simple, straightforward, grateful communication a habit. Let us consider doing the same.

Gratitude Feast

Dr. Barnet Meltzer, of the Meltzer Wellness Institute advices us to eat our meals in a similar meditative mindset. Rather than gobbling down our food in a hurry, he suggests savoring each bite, really tasting each delicious morsel, and feeling grateful for the health benefits of every ingredient. I have noticed that eating with an attitude of appreciation helps us make better choices for increased nutritional value in our diet, thus contributing to better health.

Daily Expressing Gratitude

We can make it a practice to tell a spouse, partner, child, coworker, or friend something we appreciate every day.

Here's an example from a friend of mine who is a real estate broker. The receptionist at the front desk in his office had gradually become grumpy and irritable, hardly ever smiling or greeting people in a cordial way. One evening my friend was pondering this unhappy situation when it dawned on him that the receptionist might be feeling unappreciated. He asked himself, "What can I do to help?" Relaxing his muscles and breathing deeply, he waited for an idea. Soon in his mind's eye, he saw himself stopping by a flower stand and buying a single flower for his receptionist. He later bought her the flower.

As he approached her desk, he handed her the flower, saying, "Thank you for everything you do. You are deeply appreciated." She looked surprised as she took the carnation, mumbled "Thanks," put it in a glass tumbler from the kitchen, and placed it on her desk. Each morning, my friend brought her a different kind of flower, which she added to the growing bouquet. After only two weeks, her disposition changed radically. Without any great fanfare, philosophical discussion, or job warning, the receptionist became pleasant and warm again, as she had been when she first started to work in the organization, and she stayed that way.

Before he passed away last year, stand-up comic George Carlin created a YouTube message for his posterity-this message encapsulates the most important lessons he had learned in his lifetime, lessons he wanted to share with us . . . the following reminders are part of his concluding remarks:

> "Remember to spend some time with your loved ones because they are not going to be around forever.
>
> Remember to say a kind word to someone who looks up to you in awe because that little person soon will grow up and leave your side.
>
> Remember to give a warm hug to the one next to you because that is the only treasure you can give with your heart and it doesn't cost a cent.
>
> Remember to say "I love you" to your partner and your loved ones, but most of all mean it. A kiss and an embrace will mend hurt when it comes from deep inside of you.
>
> Remember to hold hands and cherish the moment for someday that person will not be there again.
>
> Give time to love, give time to speak! And give time to share the precious thoughts (of gratitude) in your mind." (Carlin 2008)

Certainly, as reflected in Carlin's heartfelt advice, we know the virtue of gratitude helps build strong, positive, mutually satisfying and beneficial relationships. We can choose to enter the portal of gratitude in any moment. Gratitude helps us to live in the present, rejoice for what we have, improve our well-being and disposition, and accept ourselves and others.

Key Ideas to Remember about Gratitude

- **Gratitude**

   Gratitude is the feeling and attitude of appreciation or thankfulness for the benefits we have received or expect to receive. The feeling of genuine gratitude opens the channels for more goodness to enter into our life experience. Fortunately, it is the portal that's often easiest for many of us to enter even when love, generosity, and compassion feel blocked.

- **Gratitude as a Virtue**

   Gratitude has been said to have one of the strongest links with mental health of any character trait. We, as grateful people, make it a point to be aware of what's wonderful and successful and share our gratitude with others,

- **Unconditional Gratitude**

   When we freely express gratitude, it is akin to unconditional giving. Expressing gratitude usually increases trust, kindness, and respect in our relationships because it is offered unconditionally with no thought of receiving appreciation in return.

- **Gratitude Impacts Well-Being and Disposition**

   Feeling grateful and expressing our gratitude is not just an emotional response to an event or situation. It is truly a committed choice we make in any given context to experience greater wellness and vitality in our lives.

- **Accepting Oneself and Others**
  To forgive others, we must accept what we have done and let go of what we need to forgive. We must love all of ourselves, not just the pretty and socially acceptable parts, and consider being grateful for our whole life experience, which has guided us deftly to where we are now.

- **Reveling in the Ordinary**
  As we develop a greater appreciation for the ordinary things and experiences in our lives, we cultivate a profound sense of awe toward life itself. Respecting the similarities of our lives lets us see everything as a gift of goodness and well-being and helps us to feel gratitude.

- **Living in the Present Moment**
  Cherishing each moment and acting according to our inner wisdom opens the way for increased blessings and heightened gratitude.

- **Entering the Portal of Gratitude**
  At first, we may need a great deal of determination to remain devoted to deliberately looking for things to be grateful for every day, and such a spiritual habit is well worth cultivating. Michael Beckwith says, "The universe begins to pour things into you to be grateful for whenever you feel grateful for anything in any moment."

- **Practices for Cultivating Gratitude**
  Practice being grateful until finally the disposition of gratitude is a deeply ingrained habit. These practices

include keeping gratitude inventoried or journaling about what we appreciate, making a mentor list, writing gratitude notes or letters, taking gratitude walks, and turning meals into gratitude feasts.

- **Daily Expressing Gratitude**
  To complete the gratitude and practice, express our feelings and thoughts of appreciation to others, simply say, "Thank you" when such expression is sincere and genuine.

CHAPTER 4

Compassion

*The Dalai Lama suggests, "If you want others to
be happy, practice compassion; if you want to be
happy practice compassion."
(Dreams of a Mild Mannered Hero)*

Compassion

COMPASSION IN THE LOVE, GENEROSITY, gratitude, and
compassion LGGC model can be accessed whenever we see
people going through challenging experiences. Compassion
indicates a feeling and regard of genuine empathy and
supportiveness. The Latin roots of the word compassion (*com
+ passus*) translate as "to bear or pass with" as in "to suffer with."
Words synonymous with compassion are commiseration,
mercy, tenderness, and clemency. To bear with others as they
are passing through difficulties, misfortune, trauma, pain,
distress, or suffering certainly requires patience, kindness,
and empathic awareness. Compassion is "more vigorous than

empathy alone" in that compassion "gives rise to an active desire to alleviate another's suffering."

Compassion is a fundamental virtue in all of the world's major faith and wisdom traditions. In both Judaism and Islam, God is called "the Compassionate" and "the Merciful." In the Torah, God is invoked as the "Father of Compassion." All but one of the 114 chapters of the Koran begins with the verse, "In the name of God the Compassionate, the Merciful." Not only in the Jewish and Muslim traditions but in Christianity also, compassion and mercy are synonymous with the concept of the highest value, the notion of God itself.

One of the most-often-quoted parables in the Bible from Matthew 22 is that of the good Samaritan, which arose out of a question-and-answer session between Jesus and a lawyer. The lawyer asked Jesus what he needed to do to inherit eternal life. In reply, Jesus asked what the lawyer's understanding of the law was on this point. The learned lawyer answered, "You shall love the Lord your God with all your heart, with all your soul, with all your strength, and with your entire mind; and your neighbor as yourself." "Right!" said Jesus.

But then the lawyer wanted to know the definition of a neighbor. Jesus replied by relating a story about a Jewish man who had been beaten and robbed and left to die on a dangerous incline called "the Bloody Pass" on the road to Jericho. Both a priest and a Levite came along but crossed over to the other side of the road, hurrying on and ignoring the suffering man. Then came along a Samaritan, a member of an ethnic group looked down upon by the Jews. Not only did he go over to the see what the man's condition was, but:

> "He was moved with compassion and bound up his wounds, pouring on oil and wine. He set him on his own animal, and brought him to an inn, and took care of him. On the next day, when he departed, he took out two denarii, and gave them to the host, saying, "Take care of him. Whatever you spend beyond that, I will repay you when I return." Then Jesus asked the lawyer who out of these three was the true neighbor, to which the lawyer replied: "He who showed mercy."

Additionally, Martin Luther King Jr. used this parable to make a point about compassion and courage in his final talk, "I've Been to the Mountaintop," delivered on the day before his assassination. He suggested that perhaps the priest and the Levite were afraid that the man on the side of the road might be faking his injuries as a lure for robbers to attack them. Thus the priest and the Levite passed by without helping or even going over to see what was wrong. The Samaritan had the courage and kindness to help the beaten man even in the midst of the possibility of attack. King said, "And so the first question that the priest asked, the first question that the Levite asked was, 'If I stop to help this man, what will happen to me?' But then the Good Samaritan came by, and he reversed the question: 'If I do not stop to help this man, what will happen to him?'" That is compassion!

Most great religions of the world agree that the way to heaven is by being kind, compassionate, helpful, or a true neighbor to all. In Aramaic, the language spoken in biblical times, the word *hell* meant separation and isolation, whereas the word *heaven* meant togetherness and oneness. Rumi writes, "Go my friend—bestow your love, even on your foes. If you touch their hearts, what do you think will happen?" Being compassionate allows us to experience the oneness of ourselves with others, to dissolve the false appearance of separation.

When we are aware that we are all one integrated being, we have reached the stage of true compassion where no boundaries create an illusion of separation between people. Compassion is necessary to achieve emotional maturity. It is through compassion that a person achieves the highest peak and deepest reach in his or her search for self-fulfillment.

How does compassion enrich our lives? We feel peace and happiness in our own lives when we have helped others evolve to greater peace. In our relationships, we feel an expanded sense of spaciousness when we treat each other with compassion.

Compassion as a Virtue

When people think about how to treat one another, the Golden Rule often comes to mind. The Golden Rule compels us to do unto others as we would have them do unto us. The word *do* is pivotal here, not just think of or feel toward others as we would have them think or feel toward us. Together, thinking, feeling, and doing are all vital aspects that form the complete principle of compassion. Activating the virtue of compassion is the cornerstone of positive social interconnection and humanism.

Compassion's Reward

The law of compensation, from Ralph Waldo Emerson, says that whatever action we take eventually comes back to us in precise and equal measure. This law, which functions in our personal human sphere and throughout the universe, maintains a steady state of equilibrium through the give and take of energy. The compensatory result, the reward, of treating ourselves and others with compassion is that we feel happy and contented in our hearts, knowing we are helping humanity evolve to greater peace and harmony. Surely we are creating our own futures by our actions and treatment of people today. There is a valuable saying which states, *"How others treat us is their karma, and how we treat them is ours!"*

Compassion's Spaciousness in Relationships

Certainly, a sense of spaciousness is felt in relationships characterized by compassion. Compassion is that airy, spacious quality that nurtures our relationships and lets us respect and serve each other in the midst of all our differences. That's why I think the image of a soft, gentle breeze symbolizes this noble quality. With compassion, we respect each other's differences, giving each other room to grow and to live. The *Tao Te Ching* a Chinese classic text, says that it is the emptiness or the space of an enclosure that is useful. The interior space of a cooking pot allows us to boil water in the pot. The space or silence between the individual tones in music creates its melody and rhythm.

Nonjudgment in Compassion

Dr. Ernest S. Holmes founder of Religious Science is a brilliant speaker, a gifted thinker and an inspired writer. His message is very basic and simple. He states, "The universe has intelligence, purpose, and order. By understanding its principles and applying them to ourselves, we can see who we are and what we truly want in life. "Creative Mind "was written as a simple guide for the many thousands who came to hear his words and wished to know more." Dr. Holmes is also one of the founders of the New Thought Movement which became popular in the early twentieth century. Yet another valuable thought that can be attributed to him is, "if for none other than purely selfish reasons alone, we simply cannot afford to be critical of anyone." By criticizing someone, we are essentially criticizing the spirit of life itself that has taken form in this person. Moreover, when criticizing life, we are criticizing ourselves since we are one with life. When criticizing others, we are removing contentment and genuine happiness from within. If we don't like the feeling of being condemned, we must not condemn ourselves or anyone else. (Holmes 1957).

Condemnation and other degrees of judgment block our feeling and expression of compassion. When we see a homeless man, are we quick to judge that person? Do we ever take time to get to learn about someone who is different or who obviously has challenges?

Once during a visit to Texas, I was sitting next to a young man at a lunch counter at a coffee shop. I overheard him asking the waitress how much a bowl of soup cost. The sincerity and plaintive tone of his voice touched my heart. I could see he was hungry, yet he couldn't afford to buy the soup. Without saying anything, I slipped a five-dollar bill under his napkin, and we glanced at each other. He nodded silently and ordered the soup. Afterward, as we happened to be leaving at the same time, I asked him if he had a moment to talk. "I'm free till around dinner time," he answered. We found a place in a park nearby to sit down while he told me his life's story.

Twenty-five years ago, he was an innocent little kid who was often abused sexually by his mother's boyfriend. After she broke up with him, she found another boyfriend, who she supported with a meager welfare check each month. The new boyfriend would beat him up repeatedly, finally kicking him out of his mother's apartment. The young boy found a temporary job right away in a warehouse, but a heavy package fell and crushed his foot, so he was immediately fired. After he could walk again, he worked at a series of odd jobs. He was never able to keep a steady job due to the shifting nature of unskilled labor. Plus, with his disabled foot, he found that work was difficult under circumstances that called for physical stamina and strength. Anytime he could, he continued to work now and then whenever possible, at least temporarily until he became homeless. He also said to me, "Poverty isn't just living on welfare. It's when you live from one meal to the next, not knowing where you're going to sleep that night."

Too often we look with disdain or loathing upon people with situations such as this man's. We hear people say, "Let them get a job like everyone else. We shouldn't enable their laziness by giving handouts" or "We're just weakening them further by giving them money or food" or "He's probably a drug addict or alcoholic anyway, so our good money is being thrown to the bad" or "He probably has a stash of money hidden away somewhere—probably has more money than I do."

There may certainly be a measure of truth in these statements, and perhaps some people in seemingly desperate circumstances may be better off than they appear. What I honestly think is that we should not approach our fellow beings with a preprogrammed agenda, judgment, or belief about their condition and character. In instances when we notice someone needing help, we should take a moment to go within and ask for guidance and then follow that intuitive guidance on giving something to the person or not. Checking into the interior universal wisdom on a case-by-case basis allows us to do the most authentically compassionate thing, the most life-expanding action for both of us. Judging others is not only harming the person we are judging but making our own inner experience of life empty and dry.

Compassionate Empathy

When we are nonjudgmental toward others, we are able to focus on the needs of others. Empathy toward others is the heightened sense of awareness, partial identification with the feelings of another, and insight into his/her life that led to the present condition. Through the eyes and heart of empathy, we begin to gain entrance into the other person's perspectives, values, beliefs, feelings, or actions. We may not agree with attitudes or like their actions, but we can at least glimpse into what life must be like when seen and felt from their perspective.

Empathetic people really listen and put away their own concerns. They also notice the subtle verbal and nonverbal signals people express that communicate wants and needs. Fortunately, the skills of expanded awareness and empathy can be taught. A Canadian nonprofit group called Roots of Empathy, founded by retired teacher Mary Gordon, and has been training children from kindergarten through eighth grade in empathy. The classroom children observe the emotional reactions of "empathy babies" to various behaviors of the parents or others. The teacher encourages the students to detect how the baby must be feeling based on his/her appearance and reactions.

Over the past decade, Roots of Empathy training has been taking place at schools in Canada, Australia, New Zealand, and the United States with more than 6,200 empathy babies and 158,000 students thus far. The findings are astounding. Generally a consistent drop in aggressive behavior was observed among the students involved in the empathy training classes. Results of a seven-year study at the University of British Columbia showed 88 percent less bullying behavior among students who were in an "empathy baby" classroom as compared with students who were not. Children exposed to the Roots of Empathy training tend to recognize and talk about their own feelings instead of acting them out aggressively, thus increasing their emotional literacy through self-awareness and awareness of others' feelings.

Direct contact with those from backgrounds different from ours is very valuable for increasing our empathy. Some believe if there had been a Jewish person in every German household, a holocaust would never have occurred. Yet even without direct contact, we can still cultivate a general feeling of human connection at spiritual and emotional levels through being committed to expanding our empathy and sense of oneness with all beings.

Compassionate people are merciful. To show mercy, we can't go around hating, blaming and criticizing, or killing each other. When we are negative, the principle of compassion remains only a good idea, like a tiny seed lying dry and alone on a shelf—only a possibility or potential. Thomas Troward, the brilliant English philosopher early in the twentieth century, said that in order to exist as a substantial entity at all, anything must have both an inside and an outside. The inside of compassion is the idea and feeling of mercy, kindness, empathy, and oneness. The outside of compassion is the practical application, the action that issues forth in our relationships with others and all life. Compassion emerges as helpfulness, generous support, and loving-kindness, tenderness of tone and speech (courtesy), and deep listening from a heart of nonjudgment. More virtuous than simple empathy, compassionate empathy gives rise to an active desire to alleviate another's suffering.

Looking for Hidden Stories

To alleviate suffering and cultivate compassion in our lives, one of the first things we do is expand our awareness of what's happening in our environment. So many times, we rush around more or less oblivious of what other people are facing in their lives. Too often we stay enclosed within a relatively limited perspective of life by focusing on our own personal problems, needs, activities, and desires. These needs are certainly important and are not to be downplayed. Many counselors and spiritual advisors, as in the Buddhist and Sufi traditions, offer an effective way to lift ourselves out of self-absorption with our own struggles, discouragement, and depression. They suggest enlarging the circumference of our awareness to include challenges other people are going through or facing.

For instance, we pass the staff in hotel hallways behind the heavy vats of laundry they are pushing along. We may not even notice them at all, as though they were like the fixtures or plants in the background. Taking a moment to smile and greet them or thank them for making everything so beautiful and clean is not difficult. These simple expressions ease both of our hearts by allowing us to be connected to others, even if only briefly. Why do we withhold these gentle touches of humanity and connection from each other?

At work we may encounter people who are successful, intelligent, and kind. Yet something about these seemingly successful people seems a "little off." We can take time to look deeper into those around us in our environment. Even when the outer appearance seems beautiful or happy, there is always more hidden beneath the surface. For example, a wealthy colleague of mine lived with her husband in a lovely suburb of San Francisco. As she took her leisurely evening walk around the neighborhood, she would look at the houses and glance into the windows and see people laughing, sharing dinner, or just sitting in their living rooms chatting in front of a roaring fire. To her, these neighbors looked so content. Also, her own home from the outside appeared nice and filled with joy and beauty.

But a secret hid behind those walls and doors. Her husband, who had been out of work for some time, was extremely anxious and angry. He often drank too much and then lost his temper. He attacked her verbally, or hit and shoved her in a fit of rage. She kept thinking things would change if he could only get a job, but the physical abuse was progressively worsening. One night, after he had punched her in the face, the police came to the door because neighbors had called them after hearing screaming and crashing sounds. Even when help arrived, my colleague tried to protect the image of a happy marriage by telling the police she had lost her footing and fallen down the staircase.

After her son turned eighteen, my colleague made the wise decision to move across the country to end the abuse. Her sister responded to her and her situation with compassion. Even though it was not easy or convenient, she allowed my friend to come and live with her in a safe and sane environment.

Not only in our everyday lives but also when traveling, we can examine our environment for opportunities to share compassion or respond compassionately when a situation warrants. A few years ago, I was at a national conference, which was being held at a four-star hotel in Chevy Chase, Maryland. On the second day, I dashed up to my room to get a book and other things that I needed. As I entered the open doorway, I heard the sound of sobbing coming from inside. I hesitated briefly, not wanting to intrude, but since I needed my items, I decided to enter. From the bathroom, I could hear someone crying. Then a young woman stepped out, looked at me with embarrassment, and apologized. She said she didn't want to disturb me and would return to finish cleaning the room later. After assuring her that she was not disturbing me, I asked, "Do you need help?" as I reached for my wallet to give her some money. "Oh no, that's not it," she said. "My son in the Dominican Republic is extremely ill, and he may not survive according to the doctors. I haven't seen him in eight years, and I might not be able to ever see him again." I told her I was truly sorry to hear this and asked if there was anything I could do. She said she felt better just being able to tell me of her sorrow. Are we willing to take time to listen compassionately to the sorrows or concerns of those around us or even strangers?

Every person has a story. If we can just remember to listen, we can proceed without criticism and blame and maintain an open sense of well-wishing, respect, and kind regard—important characteristics of true compassion.

Personal Compassion

Even when we do become more sensitive to the plight of others through expanding our empathic awareness, we don't always respond by taking action to help in some practical way. Keep in mind, empathetic actions can be as simple as smiling, listening quietly, or holding a hand. A warm, caring smile can transmit a silent message of connection and kindness. Such a smile can be sent to the cashier who rings up our purchases, our child's teacher, the office clerk who greets us, the person collecting charitable donations, a passerby on the sidewalk, and our children, family, friends, and partners.

We often get so wrapped up in our private worries and thoughts that we lose sight of what our facial expressions are conveying to others. On the way to school, a daughter of a friend of mine used to say to her mother, "Why are you angry, Mom?" Her mother would say, "Angry? I'm not angry. What made you think that?" The child would say, "You were frowning, and I thought maybe I had done something to make you mad."

Conversely, a gentle smile, even when we're not saying anything to a child, carries a feeling of being loved and delighted in creating memories of closeness and being valued. School psychologists say that it's important not to have arguments or fights with our children in the morning before school, especially on the day of a big test. Such negative emotional situations interfere with the child's ability to concentrate and handle the stress of a demanding exam, consequently lowering the little one's academic performance. Next time we are tempted to frown, burst out in anger, or show irritation, disappointment, or disapproval, let us keep quiet and save the conversation for a better time when we're no longer upset, and instead, *smile*! If necessary, say something like, "We'll talk about this later when we're both feeling better." The results will be amazing.

Dr. Robert Simon, is an expert psychologist. He often works with suicidal patients. In an E-source article, *Just a Smile and a Hello on the Golden Gate Bridge*, he asks some insightful questions such as, "When we smile and say hello to strangers or strangers smile at us, what mental communication takes place? What do we feel in either situation? Are we making a human connection that closes our separateness, even for a moment?" Dr. Simon refers to Emile Durkheim, who in his early study of suicide, identified social isolation and impersonality ("anomie") as contributing factors to suicide. "A smile may puncture the lethal bubble of isolation and loneliness that often precedes suicide," comments Dr. Simon. "Perhaps a smile may convey the message, 'You are a valued person. I respect your being. Live!' I also wonder if, in some instances, a smile stirs veiled, primal memories of a parent's loving smile. We should not overlook the power of the simple human connection contained in a smile, even a smile between strangers." What are the other actions we can take as empathic people? (Simon 2013).

Certainly, we convey and circulate our empathy and compassion through the simple acts of listening and of using kind and supportive words. Whether it's a conversation with a friend, family member, partner, worker, teacher, or perfect stranger whom we will never see again, we owe them and ourselves the gift of really listening. Unfortunately, too often our preconceptions, assumptions, beliefs, and judgments interfere with our ability to hear what the other person is saying. Once I had a physics professor who didn't bathe often and always wore shabby clothes. At first, most of his students had a hard time listening to his lectures and discounted his knowledge because they were put off by his disheveled appearance. Finally as the prejudgment lessened, we started hearing the brilliance and subtlety of his explanations. As a result, we learned more about this physical universe at the mysterious level of the invisible than we could have done had we persisted in blinding prejudice and deafening expectations.

The harm of not listening and of speaking cruelly or sarcastically definitely wreaks havoc in our lives. Time and energy are wasted when we don't listen or filter what the other person is saying through our own preconceptions and bias. No authentic communication or connection is possible under such circumstances. Conflicts in the home or workplace often happen because people don't listen well. Furthermore, harsh words and condemnation block peace and love and are in opposition to compassion.

Applying true compassion in our own families and personal relationships is even more difficult when deep-seated anguish is present. Such anguish may be borne from psychological, emotional, and often addiction-related problems. In every relationship, whether or not substance abuse is involved, the habit of blaming others for our situation is indeed deadly. By blaming anyone or anything for any mess in our lives, we are only delaying our own evolution toward a happier life. When we point outside ourselves for the cause, we are refusing to take responsibility for our own actions. When we take responsibility for whatever happens in our lives, we need to remember not to blame or judge ourselves harshly either. In the spirit of honoring and respecting, we assess, discern, and understand a situation in a positive, flexible, resilient, and forward-moving way. That way we keep open avenues for further growth toward harmony, peace, love, and joy in our personal and professional relationships.

Basically communication is a skill we learn and practice with deliberate intention to foster relationships that are positive and enriching. Artful communication is not something with which we are born. Indeed, a baby normally cries and screams when it wants something. A toddler may whine and throw a tantrum even though we urge her/him to use words. Older children may lie or sneak around to get what they want rather than using simple requests in a direct manner. Fortunately, as we grow and mature, we may consciously and conscientiously cultivate the skill of artful communication. A skillful conversation is characterized by the five traits: 1) timeliness; 2) truthfulness; 3) gentleness; 4) purposefulness; and 5) kindness.

Courtesy Circulates Compassion

Courtesy is defined as a respectful act or expression of behavior marked by respect for others. Courtesy is also showing of politeness in one's attitude and behavior toward others, or kindness and consideration expressed in a sophisticated and elegant way. Gary Chapman, an internationally respected marriage and family life expert, says that courtesy, which is "the act of treating everyone as a personal friend," is rooted in the belief that everyone is worthy and valuable. Treating all others with polite speech and manners circulates caring compassion and stimulates positive and enriching feelings of appreciation and human connection. Chapman urges us to remember that "behind every face is a struggling human spirit." The struggle can be from physical pain, illness, difficult relationship situations, or financial stress. Most of the time we will not be aware of the nature of the hidden struggle, but we may be sure that everyone with whom we interact on any given day will be dealing with some kind of struggle. (Chapman 2009).

Whether we are interacting with a stranger, coworker, friend, or family member, we are experiencing a little slice of life, even if for only a few moments. We may disagree with his/her opinions or dislike his/her actions. In those few moments, we have the choice of connecting through courtesy or withdrawing through rudeness and disdain. If we make a commitment to activate the powerful energy of compassion in our lives and make it a part of our legacy, we shall seek to develop the habit of treating all others with courtesy.

Gary Chapman suggests a useful exercise to many of his clients during counseling sessions. Write the following five facts of human reality on an index card. Then think of someone who's hard for you to be courteous to, and say the sentences aloud with the person's name as the subject of each brief sentence:

1. All people are valuable.
2. All people have the potential to be a part of positive relationships.

3. All people are struggling.
4. All people need love.
5. All people are enriched by courtesy.

Afterward we will be able to feel the softening, opening effect in our attitudes and feelings toward this person.

Community Compassion

Action may lend itself to compassionate, humanitarian goodness for the benefit of a community. Seeing with the eyes of compassion characterizes the triumph of Scott Neeson, who, in 2003, founded the Cambodian Children's Fund (CCF). Scott gave up his career as a successful Hollywood film executive to run the fledgling organization in Phnom Penh. The CCF program offers protection, health care, education, and vocational training for children, most of whom are full-time residents at the CCF schools. Many of the children came from Stung Meanchey, Phnom Penh's garbage dump, where they worked every day picking through the garbage for items to sell. Without schooling, health care, and basic human services, these children have almost no chance of escaping poverty and crime. The children in CCF are sponsored by generous donors around the world who interact individually (e.g., mail, e-mail) and offer financial support. The children develop life-affirming, nurturing relationships with these donors, thus helping to break long generations of poverty and abuse in this ancient country. The successful efforts of organizations such as the CCF is reminiscent of

Mahatma Gandhi's often-mentioned maxim when he taught his followers that "serving others is serving God."

Global Compassion

Another powerful, contemporary story of compassion is that of Azim Khamisa, author of books including *From Murder to Forgiveness* and *From Forgiveness to Fulfillment*. Azim's twenty-year-old son was fatally shot by a fourteen-year-old gang member in January 1995 while he was attempting to deliver pizzas. At first when he received news of his son's murder, Azim felt like a nuclear bomb had exploded in his chest, draining his life force. Then he went into an altered state of consciousness in which he experienced himself being held in the arms of his God. "There, in that state of peace, I realized a profound truth—an idea so far removed from a normal reaction to my son's murder that to others it would seem inconceivable. What was this knowledge that I instantaneously embraced? Simply this: There were victims at both ends of the gun."

Through this insight bolstered by his meditation practices, grief rituals, and his Ismaili Sufi spiritual tradition, Azim transformed his horror into forgiveness and empathy for the young murderer and his family. He established a foundation in his son's name that teaches nonviolence and forgiveness in hundreds of schools across the United States and beyond. Over the past seventeen years, the Tarik Khamisa Foundation has presented thousands of creative, interactive programs to millions of youths and their parents with the purpose of "stopping kids from killing kids." Azim and the murderer's grandfather have been working together as brothers along with all the volunteers and staff of the foundation's multiple programs. These programs guide children and adults in the ways of achieving inner peace while becoming a generation of peacemakers out in the community.

Azim Khamisa turned the tragedy of losing his beloved son into compassionate, humanitarian service at the global level. The way to live a life of deep purpose and fulfillment, he writes, is "by choosing a path of peace, by letting go of negative, hurtful emotions, and by sowing your own seeds of transformation through empathy, compassion, goodwill, and forgiveness. It is by living a life of love—self-love and love for others—that we will find our own spiritual purpose, for it cannot be found in the darkness. It can only be found in the light." It is possible to take our pain and turn it inside out to help others. Compassionate intent combined with action can allow us to make a significant, positive impact on mankind. (Khamisa 1998).

Entering the Portal of Compassion

By imagining the LGGC model and choosing to be consciously impacted with compassionate awareness, we can deeply experience the sacredness of life. When we enter the compassion portal, we can feel enlivened and warm and have our priorities clarified. Once we clarify our priorities, we can decide how we want to serve, genuinely communicate, and facilitate compassionate connections in every area of our lives.

Daily Expressing Compassion

We can express compassion in our daily lives by living with nonjudgment, looking for hidden stories, taking action in our words and humanitarian service, listening to others, having empathy, and being quietly patient and courteous. In the Buddhist tradition, compassion is considered the antidote to the self-administered poison of anger. Ananda, the Buddha's personal attendant, is said to have asked: "Wouldn't it be true to say that the cultivation of loving-kindness and compassion is part of our practice?" to which, the Buddha replied: "No, it would not be true to say that the cultivation of loving-kindness and compassion is part of our practice. It would be true to say that the cultivation of loving-kindness and compassion is all of our practice."

As the fourth portal of LGGC, compassion is the result of activity in all the other portals and the gateway into them as well. Without compassion, we experience life as sterile, lonely, and dangerous. With compassion, we feel safe and valuable as integral and necessary beings in the ongoing evolution of humanity. Compassion enables us to intimately experience the oneness and divinity of all life.

Key Ideas to Remember About Compassion

- **Compassion**
  Compassion indicates a feeling and regard of genuine empathy and supportiveness to another in need.

- **Compassion as a Virtue**
  Activating the virtue of compassion is what establishes it as the cornerstone of positive social interconnection and humanism.

- **Compassion's Reward**
  The reward of treating ourselves and others with compassion is that we feel contented in our hearts, knowing we are helping humanity evolve to greater peace and harmony.

- **Compassion's Spaciousness in Relationships**
  Compassion is that airy, spacious quality that nurtures our relationships and lets us respect and serve each other in the midst of all our differences.

- **Nonjudgment in Compassion**
  Condemnation and other degrees of judgment block our feeling and expression of compassion.

- **Compassionate Empathy**
  We as compassionate, empathetic people are able to really listen to and understand the experiences other people describe.

- **Looking for Hidden Stories**
  We can enlarge the circumference of our awareness to include the challenges other people are going through or facing.

- **Personal Compassion**
  We can demonstrate compassion in empathetic actions as simple as smiling, listening quietly, or holding a hand.

- **Courtesy Circulates Compassion**
  Treating all others with polite speech and manner, we circulate caring compassion and stimulate positive and enriching feelings of appreciation and human connection.

- **Community Compassion**
  Action may lend itself to compassionate, humanitarian goodness for the benefit of a community.

- **Global Compassion**
  Compassionate intent combined with action can allow us to make a significant, positive impact on mankind.

- **Enter the Portal of Compassion**
  When we enter the portal of compassion, we can feel enlivened and warm and receive clarification of our priorities.

- **Daily Expressing Compassion**
  We can express compassion in our daily lives by living with nonjudgment, looking for hidden stories, taking action in our words, listening to others, having empathy, and being quietly patient and courteous.

CONCLUSION

RECALL THE NOTE MY MOTHER jotted down in her diary expressing her love for me mentioned in the introduction. This is her legacy for me. I strongly recommend that we all leave behind something similar in writing for our children and loved ones. This would be a tangible reminder of our love and affection for them after we are gone. This is a precious gift worth leaving as a source of joy; or as in my case the greatest source of strength knowing that I was loved unconditionally.

The circle of LGGC is a very powerful symbol that surrounds us and has no beginning or end. Our legacy encompasses this circle. To achieve true happiness, our attitude and choices that fall within the bounds of the legacy circle lead to moments of happiness in our lives. The more we choose to live within this circle, the more moments of happiness we have. The legacy circle is within everyone's reach, and living the legacy costs nothing. Without a doubt, the return from living the legacy is immeasurable. Those we touch with our newfound love, generosity, gratitude, and compassion will soon return these virtues to us or others.

Choices outside of the legacy circle will lead to discontent, regret, arguments, conflict, and lack of appreciation for the precious lives we are given. My hope is that we will live the good life and not have to learn the hard way from crisis.

Living the legacy may not be easy at first, and new habits of generosity and gratitude may take time. One by one, I encourage us to continuously incorporate our highest virtues into our lives in very plain and practical ways. My hope is that we will make conscious choices to enter the LGGC portals and practice affirmations that will change our lives for the better. Such an affirmation may be spoken aloud or read silently. Here is a sample affirmation adapted from an ancient one.

> *May I be filled with loving-kindness.*
> *May I be generous.*
> *May I be grateful.*
> *May I be compassionate.*
> *May I be happy.*

Also, the "I" can be replaced with anyone's name.

To be happy, it is important to take a look at our attitudes toward love, generosity, gratitude, and compassion (and any other values we profess). One by one, I encourage us to check into our attitudes toward what we claim as our highest virtues to make sure we continuously incorporate them into our lives in very plain and practical ways. If we want to be more loving, generous, grateful, and compassionate but are conflicted, what is blocking the flow? Is it fear, anger, confusion, resentment, or any other negative factor? We can ask where that feeling came from and ask if the thought is still true or even useful today. If the thought is not true or useful, reject it. If it is true, does that thought bring happiness? If not, choose to enter any of the portals in the LGGC model, and then take action.

We need to take action because time and people are so precious. If we were to die today, what would we leave behind for our family, friends, and the world to know us by? What is our legacy? In each successive moment, we can be aware of the divine evolution that's going on via every single choice that we make. Our choices will eventually be part of the legacy we leave behind.

When we think of our legacy, do we want to leave behind tangible gifts, like money, houses, cars, and jewelry? These gifts are nice and beneficial, but one day, they could turn to dust.

Or when we think of our legacy, do we want to leave behind resources that can truly change people's lives for the better? If we give love, gratitude, generosity, and compassion, we can share more than money can buy. We can right now express these virtues and as a consequence leave behind that which will positively and profoundly impact us, our loved ones, and mankind for many generations.

This particular combination (LGGC) of virtues can become our motto. The virtues can be displayed on a desktop, in a calendar, on a wall, or in a cubicle. More than a motto, living by these virtues, regardless of faith, cultural tradition, career, status, family situation, sexual orientation, or physical condition, will change lives for the better.

I encourage you to meditate on the values of LGGC . . .

Love . . .
Generosity . . .
Gratitude . . .
Compassion . . .

Enter one of these portals at any given moment.

The following set of affirmations will help in establishing a frame of mind to visualize positive and desirable outcomes of incorporating the principles discussed in this book. In reviewing and repeating these affirmations I was able to create sound vibrations of what I believe to be true. I am offering them to my readers to try them for the same effect. I recommend reflecting on these affirmations in order to enter each portal offered by LGGC. Consider them the keys to unlock the doors to Love, Gratitude, Generosity and Compassion.

Affirmations to Complete the Legacy Circle

- I choose to live within the legacy circle of Love, Generosity, Gratitude and Compassion.
- Happiness abounds for me and for all, because of this choice and I am committed to it.
- Life is Good!
- I affirm love as the radiant essence of my life.
- I affirm generosity as the joyous expansion of my life.
- I affirm gratitude as the heart center of my life.
- Compassion lives within me now and forever.
- Passing along my legacy of Love, Generosity, Gratitude and Compassion I am making a profound impact in this world.
- My Life Matters!
- I live up to the highest and best ideals I am able to perceive, which exist within me.
- Entering these portals allows me to live an inspired life and I hereby bequeath my Legacy
- Of Love, Generostiy, Gratitude and Compassion to All!

And so it is . . .

REFERENCE SOURCES

(Alphabetical)

Introduction

Angelou, Maya. (2010). *Be Yourself Inspirational Quotes* URL: http:// www.pinterest.com/runamongus/be-yourself-inspirational quotes/ (Accessed February 8, 2013)

Covey, Stephen R. (1989). *The Seven Habits of Highly Effective People*. New York, New York. Free Press. pp. 96-97

Fox, Emmet. (1946). *Make Your Life Worthwhile*. New York, New York. Harper Collins. pp. 95-96.

Gilman, William H; Ferguson; George; Merrell R. Davis. (1960). *Journals and Miscellaneous Notebooks of Ralph Waldo Emerson, Volume I: 1819-1822*. Boston, Massachusetts. Harvard University Press.

Kornfield. Jack. (2010) *Guided Meditations for Difficult Times: A Lamp in the Darkness*. (Audio book and CD). Louisville, Colorado. Sounds True Inc.

Njoku, Ugo. (2011). *Free Your Mind*. Nigeria, Africa. Seeds in Words (E-source). URL: http://www.seedsinwords.com/about-these-seeds/ (accessed February 8, 2013).

Chapter One-Love

Baer, Greg. (2003). *Real Love: The Truth About Finding Unconditional Love and Fulfilling Relationships*. New York, New York. Putnam, Penguin Publishing.

Beckwith, Michael (Rev.) (2013). *The Inspirit Center for Spiritual Living*. (E-source) URL: http://agapelive.com/index.php?page=3 (retrieved February 7, 2013).

Bennet, Sage (Rev.) (2007). *Wisdom Walk: Nine Practices for Creating Peace and Balance From the World's Spiritual Traditions*. Novato, California. New World Library.

Chapman, Gary. (2009). *Love as a Way of Life: Keys to Transforming Every Aspect of Your Life*. New York, New York. Random House Publishers.

De Angelis, Barbara. (E-source) URL:http//www.brainyquotes.com

Emoto, Dr. Masaru. (2004) *The Hidden Message of Water*. Hillsboro, Oregon. Beyond Words Publishing Inc.

Flesch, Rudolf. (1957). *The Book of Unusual Quotations.* New York, New York. Harper & Brothers Publishers.

Hahn, Thich Nhat. (2005). *Being Peace.* Berkeley, California. Parallax Press.

Holy Bible. King James Version. (E-source) URL. http://www.o-bible.com/kjv.html. (accessed February 6, 2013).

Jampolsky, Dr. Gerald G. (2004). *Love is Letting go of Fear.* Berkeley, California. Celestial Arts Publishing.

Lokos, Allen. (2012). *The Art of Peaceful Living.* New York, New York. Penguin Books. Schwartz, Daylee Deanna (2012) (E-book).
URL: http://howdoiloveme.com/the_book/

Smith, Dr. River. (2009). *A Conspiracy to Love: Living a Life of Joy, Generosity and Power.* Cleveland, Ohio. Satyagraha-Create Space Publishing.

Tetteh, Ismael. (2005). The Way Forward: Principles and Practices for Empowered Living. Ghana, Africa. Etherean Mission Publishing.

Chapter Two-Generosity

Beckwith, Michael (Rev.) (2013). *The Inspirit Center for Spiritual Living.* (E-source) URL: http://agapelive.com/index.php?page=3 (retrieved February 7, 2013).

Castaneda, Carlos. (1969). The *Teachings of Don Juan: A Yaqui Way of Knowledge.* Berkeley, California. University of California Press.

Definition-**Generosity.** (E-definitions) URL: http://www.definitions.net/definition/generosity.

Holy Bible. King James Version. (E-source) URL. http://www.o-bible.com/kjv.html. (accessed February 6, 2013).

Khan, Salman. *The Khan Academy*-YouTube Video URL://http://www.youtube.com/user/khanacademy/ (accessed February 7, 2013).

Maathai Wangari. (20130. Biographical". *Nobelprize.org.* Nobel Media AB http://www.nobelprize.org/nobel_prizes/peace/laureates/2004/maathai-bio.html (accessed February 7, 2013).

Outler, Albert, C. (1987) *John Wesley's Sermons: An Anthology.* Nashville, Tennessee. Abington Press.

Rand D.G. J.D. Greene & M.A. Nowak. (2012). *Spontaneous Giving and Calculated Greed: Nature. (*489, 427-430, (20 September 2012), doi:10.1038/nature11467) Program for Evolutionary Dynamics, Harvard University, Cambridge, Massachusetts 02138, USA. Published online 19 September 2012
URL: http://www.nature.com/nature/journal/v489/n7416/full/nature11467.html

Roy, Sanjit "Bunker". Deepak & Bunker Event, February 4th, NYC.
URL: http://www.barefootcollege.org/about/newsroom/

Tan, Enoch. *Law of Circulation: Flow of Giving and Receiving. (E-source)* Mind Reality.
URL: http:// www.enochtan.com/mindreality/law-of-circulation-flow-of-giving.

Chapter Three-Gratitude

Arrien, Angeles Dr. (2011). *Living in Gratitude: A Journey That Will Change Your Life.* (Google eBook).
URL:http://books.google.com/books/about/Living in Gratitude.html?id=xzk2HmHcG9

Carlin, George. (2008). *On Death-RIP.* You Tube Video
URL: http://www.youtube.com/watch?v=3PiZSFIVFiU

Clark, Heather Dawn, Rev. Clark. (2013). *Center for Spiritual Living in Capistrano Valley.* Capistrano, California.

URL: http://www.cslcv.org/ (accessed February 6, 2013).

Emmons, R. A. (2009). *Greatest of the Virtues?-Gratitude and the Grateful Personality.* Narvez, D. & D. Lapsley (Eds.) (2009). *Personality, Identity, and Character: Exploration in Moral Psychology.* New York, New York. Cambridge University Press. pp. 256-270.

Emmons, R.A. & M. E. McCullough. (M.E). (2003). *Counting Blessings Versus Burdens: An Experimental Investigation of Gratitude and Subjective Well-Being in Daily Life.*

Journal of Personality and Social Psychology. Department of Psychology, 84(2) pp. 377-389.
University of California, Davis 95616, USA. Published by: Pub-Med.gov.
URL: http://www.ncbi.nlm.nih.gov/pubmed/12585811

Happy Life University
URL: http://www.happylifeu.edu (accessed February 6, 2013).

Gildenhard, Ingo. (2011). *The Construction of Reality in Cicero's Speeches. New York, New York.* Oxford University Press.

Holy Bible. King James Version. (E.source)
URL. http://www.o-bible.com/kjv.html. (accessed February 6, 2013).

Hopkins, Emma Curtis. (1888). Hopkins Scientific Christian Mental Practice.

Camarillo, California. DeVorss & Company; later printing edition (January 1, 1974)

McCullough, (M.E.) R.A. Emmons & J.A. Tsang. (2002). *The Grateful Disposition: A Conceptual and Empirical Topography.* Journal of Personality and Social Psychology. Department of Psychology, 84(2) pp. 377-389. University of California, Davis 95616, USA. Published by: Pub-Med.gov. URL: http://www.ncbi.nlm.nih.gov/pubmed/12585811

Meltzer Barnet-Meltzer Wellness Institute-*Make Time for Wellness.* URL: http://www.maketimeforwellness.com/ (accessed February 6, 2013).

Morganti, Anthony. (2011). *Quotes to Enrich Life & Spirit-From Buddha through Gandhi and Zen.* Kindle Edition. Amazon Digital Services.

Nadler, Steven. Edward N. Zalta (ed). *Baruch Spinoza.* The Stanford Encyclopedia (Fall 2012 Edition). (E-source) URL: http://plato.stanford.edu/archives/fall2012/entries/spinoza/

Price, John Randolph. (1997).*The Abundance Book.* Carlsbad, California. Hay House, Inc.

Wood, A.M. S. Joseph & J. Maltby. (2008), (2009). *Gratitude Uniquely Predicts Satisfaction With Life: Incremental Validity above the Domains and Facts of the Five Factor Model-Personality and Individual Differences pp. 45, 49-54, 655-*

660. Gratitude Influences Sleep Through the Mechanism of Pre-Sleep Cognition. pp.43-48, 66.

Chapter Four-Compassion

Chapman, Gary. (2009). *Love as a Way of Life: Keys to Transforming Every Aspect of Your Life.* New York, New York. Random House Publishers.

Dalai Lama. (2010) (E-source) URL: http//www.daily*good.org/2010/03/05/dreams-of-a-mild-mannered-hero/*

Gordon, Mary. *Roots of Empathy.* (E-source) URL:http://www.rootsofempathy.org/ (accessed February 7, 2013).

Holmes, Ernest. *New Thought Library.* (1957) (E-source). URL: http://www.newthoughtlibrary.com/holmesernest/bio_holmes.html. (accessed February 7, 2013).

Kabbalah. *Ancient Wisdom for Modern Minds.* (E-source). URL: http//www.learnkabbalaj.com/kabbalah-for-today/

Khamisa, Azim. (1998) *From Murder to Forgiveness: A Father's Journey.* Bloomington, Indiana. Balboa Press.

King, Dr. Martin J. *(Speech transcript)* I've Been to the Mountaintop.

URL:http//www.speeches-usa.com/transcripts/023_king.
html. (accessed February 7, 2013).

Koran (Qur'an). (E-source searchable version).
URL:http//www.asksam.com/ebooks/koran. (accessed
February 7, 2013).

Merton, Thomas. (1957). *The Silent Life*. New York, New York.
(Copyrighted) The Abbey of Our Lady of Gethsemane.

Mitchell, Stephen. (1988). *Tao Te Ching*. New York, New
York. Harper Collins Inc.

Neeson, Scott. *Cambodian Children's Fund (CCF)*. (E-source)
URL: http//www.cambodianchidrenfund.org/

Simon, Dr. Robert. San Diego, California. (E-source)
URL: http//simon.com/Expert Psychologist.html.

Tillich, Paul. (1952).*The Courage to Be*. New Haven,
Connecticut. Yale University Press.

Torah-*Compassion* (E-source)
URL:http//www.torah.net/

CPSIA information can be obtained at www.ICGtesting.com
Printed in the USA
BVOW02s2043181113

336664BV00001B/3/P

9 781452 580296